D1212796

THE ESSAYS OF SIR FRANCIS BACON

WITH AN INTRODUCTION

BY

CHRISTOPHER MORLEY

SIR FRANCIS BACON (1561–1626)

The Essayes

OR COUNSELS CIVILL & MORALL

OF

FRANCIS BACON

BARON OF VERULAM

VISCOUNT SAINT ALBAN

The 100 Greatest Books Ever Written

COLLECTOR'S EDITION

Bound in Genuine Leather

The Easton Press

NORWALK, CONNECTICUT

This book is printed on archival quality paper especially milled for this edition. It is acid-neutral and conforms to all guidelines established for permanence and durability by the Council of Library Resources and The American National Standards Institute. ∞™

Bacon's first group of ten *Essays* was published by Humfrey Hooper, London, in 1597; they were reprinted, together with other writings, in 1598. A volume containing nine of the original ten *Essays* and twenty-nine new ones was published in 1612. The author's complete, corrected, and final edition of fifty-eight *Essays, or Counsels Civill & Morall* was brought out in 1625. The definitive edition of Bacon's complete works, edited by R. L. Ellis *et al.*, was issued in 1857. Among the important separate editions of the *Essays* are those edited by Archbishop Whateley, 1864; Storr and Gibson, 1886; R. Wilson, 1904; and Gordon S. Haight, 1942. The complete edition including an introduction by Christopher Morley, a bibliographical note by A. S. W. Rosenbach, and a note on the text was published in New York by The George Macy Companies, Inc.

This Collector's Edition is published by advance reservation exclusively for subscribers to the Easton Press collection of *The 100 Greatest Books Ever Written.* The frontispiece portrait was specially commissioned and, like the other special contents, is

Printed in the United States of America

PUBLISHER'S PREFACE

In the annals of English literature there are two careers that run closely parallel—the careers of two men who lived in the same period and whose works are beacons of our culture. William Shakespeare's birth in 1564 followed Francis Bacon's by just three years; Shakespeare died in 1616, ten years before Bacon. And it is only a short time since people took seriously the idea that it must have been the well-educated Bacon who wrote the plays of the less-well-educated Shakespeare.

True, they both wrote beautifully, wittily, pithily, metaphorically, and both demonstrated a deep knowledge of the human heart and spirit. But there the resemblance ends.

Francis Bacon, born in York House on London's Strand, was the youngest son of Nicholas Bacon, Lord Keeper of the Great Seal of England during the reign of Queen Elizabeth. His mother was the sister-in-law of Lord Burghley, the queen's chief adviser. Francis studied the sciences taught at Trinity College, Cambridge, then went in for law and was elected to a seat in Parliament.

At the age of thirty he became confidential adviser to Elizabeth's favorite nobleman, the Earl of Essex, who presented Bacon with a piece of land near Twickenham, not far from London. But it was the budding statesman's fate that the queen required him to prepare documents against his patron when Essex was accused of treason.

After Elizabeth's death in 1603, Bacon obtained a knighthood, four years later the post of royal solicitor, and in 1613 he was appointed Attorney General. His political rise accelerated. Like his father he was appointed Lord Keeper of the Seal; in 1618 he became Lord Chancellor of England and was given the title of Baron Verulam, and in 1621 Francis Bacon was created Viscount St. Albans.

His scholarly endeavors were equally rewarding. The first ten *Essays* had been published in 1597, and republished the following year with two religious works on which he had been working. He carried on a number of scientific and philosophical investigations, hoping to become a "second Aristotle." *The Advancement of Learning*, Bacon's survey of the existing state of knowledge, came out in 1605; this and the *Novum Organum* (a "New Instrument" for interpreting nature and organizing the sciences, published in 1620) were parts of his projected major work on experimental science, but the other sections were never written. *The New Atlantis*, a Utopian fable of government, customs, and scientific study on the imaginary island of Bensalem, was published in 1627, the year after its author's death.

But Bacon had continued writing the *Essays* for which he is most widely admired, by 1612 had produced twenty-nine more, and in 1625 published the completely corrected versions of the fifty-eight *Essays, or Counsels Civill & Morall* presented in this volume. They are brief and concise, dealing in a fascinating manner—and in a highly original style—with questions mostly of personal or public conduct and with philosophical or religious matters.

Bacon's *Essays* blazed a new trail. He showed man to himself, as man really is. That was rather unorthodox, which is why Bacon is frequently called "the first modern mind." For until he wrote these *Essays* it was *religious* experience that provided poets and essayists with their subject matter. To Bacon, *natural* experience seemed more influential for the study of man. Bacon became "the Prince of Nature."

Earlier writers had regarded the physical universe as accursed, the dwelling place of Satan, where evil spirits are worshipped as Gods and Goddesses by the pagans. Francis Bacon felt that truth was to be found in things as they exist in nature. He believed that God had given two books to mankind, the Book of Revelation and the Book of Nature, and that man had neglected the second book. He developed a reverent, almost religious feeling for nature, and this gives to a great deal of his work an imaginative quality to be found later in the simple nature poetry of William Wordsworth; it became a permanent part of the English heritage.

Bacon's downfall was brought about by charges of bribery in certain important lawsuits. He confessed his technical guilt, and in 1621 was assessed a fine of £40,000, sentenced to imprisonment in the Tower of London, and deprived of his government posts; but King James remitted the fine, released him from the Tower after four days, and gave him a general pardon. Actually, as Bacon later indicated, he had never been swayed by the bribes, and his intentions had always been pure.

It was a scientific experiment that brought Bacon's life to a close (just as an electrical experiment would come close to killing a later statesman, writer, and scientist). One day in 1626, while riding in his carriage, Bacon decided to determine whether refrigeration would preserve meat from spoiling. He stopped the carriage, bought a fowl, and with his own hands helped stuff it with snow. He got a chill, caught a serious cold that resulted in bronchitis, and died after a month's illness.

In a letter written to Lord Burghley in 1592, Francis Bacon boldly asserted, "I have taken all knowledge to be my province." He never deviated from that resolve.

The introduction to this edition of the *Essays* has been written by an American whose interests were almost as far-reaching as those of Francis Bacon. Christopher Morley too is known as an essayist, and also as a novelist and journalist. Born in Pennsylvania, he was educated at Haverford College and as a Rhodes scholar at Oxford. He wrote more than fifty books. Two of them—*Parnassus on Wheels* and *The Haunted Bookshop*—are charming novels about an itinerant bookseller. Some are fantasies: *Where the Blue Begins* and *Thunder on the Left. Kitty Foyle* was Morley's most popular novel. He wrote books of amusing sketches and travel notes, humorous verse, and one-act plays. For eighteen years he was a contributing editor of *The Saturday Review of Literature*. His introduction to the present volume displays Christopher Morley's learning, his wit, his whimsicality, and a true appreciation of Bacon's *Essays*.

The book's typography is the creation of Bruce Rogers, an American equally respected on both sides of the Atlantic. After studying draftsmanship, decorative design, and the humanities at Purdue University, Rogers became interested in the arrangement of type on paper, and went to Boston to work at the Riverside Press, where he remained for seventeen years. In the course of his many visits to England he worked as Printing Adviser to the Cambridge University Press, and he served in the same capacity for Harvard University Press.

His most renowned productions include the Bruce Rogers Lectern Bible, which he designed for Oxford; a thirty-eight-volume edition of the plays and poems of Shakespeare; a limited edition of *Gulliver's Travels* in which the pages of the "Brobdingnag" volume are six times the size of those in the "Lilliput"; and *The Essays of Francis Bacon*. He was also the designer of the distinguished Centaur typeface.

The type in which these Essays are set was originally designed by Rogers for the Shakespeare set. It is based upon a type known as Janson, designed in the seventeenth century by Nicholas Kis, a Transylvanian who worked for a time at Anton Janson's typefoundry in Leipzig. The type combines a high degree of legibility with many distinctive characteristics, and its vigorous letter-forms convey to the reader's eye something of the rugged Elizabethan quality of the text. Most of the characters were redrawn by Bruce Rogers.

Decoration is brought to the page through the bold color of a large headline, set in Garamond type. The designer provided additional decoration through a series of large initial letters which he drew to begin the various essays.

For this edition a portrait of Sir Francis Bacon has been created by Richard Sparks, an artist with impressive credentials. Sparks was born in Texas in 1944 and has received degrees from Texas A & M in architecture, and from the Los Angeles Art Center College of Design in illustration. He lived and studied in Amsterdam, Holland, from 1971 to 1974 and has exhibited his works throughout Europe. He won the Gold Medal for Excellence awarded by the Society of Illustrators in 1976. Sparks maintains his home and studio in Norwalk, Connecticut.

The text has been printed on a high-quality paper stock specially made for this volume. The binding has been executed in top-grain leather. The cover design was prepared exclusively for this edition. The raised hubs on the backbone are typical of the finest hand binding. As with the other volumes in this collection of *The 100 Greatest Books Ever Written*, the page edges are protected by a decorative coating, and the beauty of the book is enhanced by its ribbon marker and moiré endleaves.

THE EASTON PRESS

INTRODUCTION

CHANCE has it that the table where I write this is covered by a sheet of glass. Through my sleeves I feel the chill of that cold slippery stuff. How I would prefer to dictate, for none can match written words with Lord Bacon. Only the humble working impromptu of live speech could stand up to that dark angel of English prose. It would be less wary than this, but more manly. Yet I feel, or have persuaded myself, that this cold plate under my elbows is somehow appropriate.

There is chill in the Essays too. It runs up the arms, it leaves one a little sick and shaken. Perhaps nowhere in literature do we more clearly see a Mind at work, and it frightens us. My Lord's Northern Lights burn and steam like dry ice; our reason is thrilled, but also (in his own words) we find we are 'full of melancholy and indisposition, and unpleasing to ourselves.' It is indeed 'a medicine too piercing and corrosive.' We have passed winter evenings with him: he had the closer ingle of the hearth, wore his furred gown, sat (I suppose) on a woolsack, firelight shone through his wineglass and his thin clerkly hands. (Little else ever slipped between his fingers.) We were catching cold but we listened to his icicle aphorisms as he bent toward the fire and talked over his shoulder. 'Rising to great place is by a winding stair,' he remarked. He suggested 'the regulating of prices of things vendible,' and added that after a war the soldiers will require 'donatives.' If we grew restless he said 'stay a little that we may make an end the sooner.' He quoted Solomon: 'Prudens advertit ad gressos suos,' and was pleased by our version, 'The wise man watches his step.' He must have heard us sneeze, for he muttered 'qui fortiter emungit, elicit sanguinem.' We tried, bashfully, to express astonishment at the frostfires of beauty that coruscate—even against his will—in the arch of his arctic sky. 'Beauty,' he mused, 'hath ever some strangeness in the proportion. It comes by a kind of felicity, and not by a rule.—But enough of these toys.'

There have been some, who had winter-talk by the fireside, or aestivated with him in that great plotted garden (what a man he was for blueprints) and came away whispering 'The old son-of-a-bitch.' That also can be true. He's like iced vermouth; lucid and orderly as a telephone book. 'The great snake,' Lytton Strachey called him in a memorable and excited passage. My Lord's retort probably was that Strachey was 'infected with the style of the poets, speaking in a perpetual hyperbole.' Others remember the smell of the mint-beds in the garden, and the wizened old chancellor treading them with his heel. So he trod out the savors of language. His abrupt felicities were all the more startling from so bony a mind. There was mustard as well as mint in that garden. He liked the mustard-seed: 'it hath a property and spirit to get up and spread.' Often he forgot our frailty and would soliloquize in Latin, old master of a double tongue. 'Qui mari potitur, eum rerum potiri,' he said (I think he was quoting Tully; or Mahan?). It was well in character that when planning his imagined country seat he specially approved bay windows —not for their view of landscape, but because they are good retiring places for conference. He was always in conference with himself.

So he usually sent us away early. 'He that is too much in anything, so that he giveth occasion of satiety, maketh himself cheap.' We always hoped to get an autograph letter from him, but he said 'It is better to deal by speech than by letter. Letters are good when a man would draw an answer by letter back again.' He paced a whole length of the mustard and watercress beds and then added, 'Or when it may serve for a man's justification afterwards to produce his own letter.'

Someone said he had seen few women of quality about the estate at St. Albans. They did not seem amused by My Lord. Probably he said once too often, 'These are but toys.' It was odd that the notion of Bacon having written Shakespeare began (or anyhow was strongly forwarded) among females. Sensitized to poets, one might expect a bluestocking to think that two more diverse minds never lived. Yet I'm not so sure. Lovers of thought have a good instinct that the essence of mind is everywhere the same. Bacon wrote his Essays young, as Shakespeare his Sonnets. The moods were completely different, but I suspect there were as many erasures when Bacon tried to say how clearly he thought as when Shakespeare tried to say how confused he felt. We are told that the Essays were revised in the last year of Bacon's life, brought down to date, after his political downfall, either as apology or as defiance. (I prefer to think the latter.) Of course no one revises sonnets. One might as well try to revise an influenza.

It would be happy—the easy happiness of scholars—to go on repeating how different were Bacon and his everlasting rival. But I don't know. I open the book almost at random, where he is dealing not with social stratagem but with doom at large. Erase a syllable here and there, reset as verse, and what have you:—

But I consent with Caesar, that the sudden
Passage is easiest; and nothing more
Awakes resolve and readiness to die
Than quiet conscience, strengthened with opinion
That we shall be well spoken-of on earth
By the just, and by the family of virtue.
The opposite is fury to a man,
Makes even life unsweet. What is more heavy
Than evil fame deserved . . . he that, yet living,
Follows the funerals of his reputation.

Would you know, old mole, who wrote it? It's from the fragment on Death, a topic even Bacon thought important enough to treat twice. To use his favorite metaphor, when great minds deal with the same theme they have their individual orbits, but are also quietly carried by the Primum Mobile. Frostbitten or not, in the Essays you will find as much of mind's Prime Movers as in anything written to the same purpose, to disregard ecstasy and convey judgement.

Like the atheism he spoke of, wisdom (even his) was more on the lip than in the heart. I wonder how he may have readjusted the Essays (to serve as mutes in the funeral of his reputation) when he revised in 1625. I suppose the existing copies (only seven, I believe) of the 1597 edition have been collated with the later volume, and experts must have noted how he rewrote.

Even for a writer of prefaces, the Essays are great preachers of brevity. His 'plausible' (viz., praiseworthy) gnomes have been copiously corroborated in all history since. In his piece on Dissimulation is a passage that might have been written as a memo for Franklin Roosevelt in 1944. You will read, I hope, not methodically but dipping here and there, sometimes pausing for the digestive chew he advised. You will find character in the fact that he is at his incomparable best on painful or executive themes—for instance, Revenge, Dissimulation, Envy, Studies,

Sedition, Cunning, Dispatch, Negotiating, Vain-Glory, Anger. Whatever you do, don't miss him on Travel. But in whatever mood, he can render as acid intellectual pleasure as print affords, and always the felicity of Lucifer. One would not praise too glibly: he pointed out, the praise of the ignorant is worth nothing.

As I write this it is snowing; one remembers the legend that a spring snowstorm killed him. He died as he lived, in a practical zeal for exact knowledge. To learn whether refrigeration really arrests decay he went outdoors to buy a drawn fowl and stuff it with snow. Maybe the Essays have kept so well, and will keep forever, for that same reason. Their entrails are packed with ice.

CHRISTOPHER MORLEY

POSTSCRIPT: Since the above was written I asked the eminent collector and scholar, Dr. A. S. W. Rosenbach, to contribute a note on the bibliography of the Essays. I am grateful to him for the appended memorandum:—

The first edition was published in 1597 and has the following title page:

> Essayes. Religious Meditations. Places of perswasion and disswasion. Seene and allowed. At London, Printed for Humfrey Hooper, and are to be sold at the blacke Beare in Chauncery Lane. 1597.

It is an octavo of 50 printed leaves and the signatures of this precious little book run A^4, B — G^8. As you know, it is one of the rarest and most desirable books in all literature. Of the seven copies known of the First Edition, the British Museum and Cambridge University Library have two copies each. In America, copies are owned by the Henry E. Huntington Library in California, and the Elizabethan Club of Yale University. Our friend Carl H. Pforzheimer has the only copy in private hands and the only one in its original binding.

The First Edition and the two issued in 1598 contain besides the literary 'Essaies,' Bacon's religious work, the 'Meditationes Sacre' and his philosophical 'The Colours of Good and Evill.' Only ten Essays appear in the sixteenth century editions and the complete edition of 58 Essays was not published until 1625, the year before Bacon's death.

There were two variants issued in 1598, one of which is known in only two copies: Trinity College, Cambridge, and the Bodleian Library, Oxford. Of the other, there are ten copies recorded. There is a very romantic story connected with the Huth copy of this issue. I bought it at the Huth Sale in London on Nov. 17, 1912, for my very dear friend Henry Elkins Widener who, if he had lived, would have been, I believe, the greatest collector the world has ever known. After the Huth Sale, young Widener slipped the volume into his pocket and turning to a friend said; 'I think I'll take that little Bacon with me in my pocket and if I'm ship-wrecked it will go down with me.' With what prophecy he spoke, they little knew! A few days later he was one of the victims of the 'Titanic' disaster.

A. S. W. Rosenbach

A NOTE ON THE TEXT

FRANCIS BACON was thirty-six years old, a member of Parliament and a bachelor, when he published the first edition of these Essays. That was in 1597. The collection of practical generalizations contained ten essays only. That it was immediately successful is proved by the fact that within a year a corrected edition appeared.

In 1612, when Bacon was fifty-one, had been married for six years and had been appointed the King's Solicitor-General, another edition was printed under his supervision. The ten essays were revised, one ('Of Honour and Reputation') was omitted, and twenty-nine new essays were added. This collection of thirty-eight essays was cherished, reprinted, and often pirated during the following decade.

In 1625, at the age of sixty-four, and when he had had many personal troubles, Bacon prepared a complete and final author's edition. In this edition the older essays, read in the light of the ripened wisdom of age, were once more critically examined and altered. Twenty new essays were added, bringing the total to fifty-eight.

The text of the present volume follows that of the edition of 1625. Of the printing of that edition Edward Arber, in his Harmony of the Essays, says, 'This impression is disfigured by a perfect eruption of capital letters, and is often cut up into almost inch lengths with commas.' Of the 1612 edition he remarks, 'This edition is distinguished by great absence of capital letters. It almost reads like a modern book.' This present printing, therefore, reverts to the style of capitalization and punctuation in the 1612 edition, for the greater convenience of the reader.

The original spelling has been scrupulously retained; but the antique usage of the letters u and v, and that of i for the more modern j, (then non-existent) have not been followed here. The long ſ also has been banished, except from the title-page.

The Table.

The Epistle Dedicatorie.

TO

THE RIGHT HONORABLE MY VERY GOOD LO.
THE DUKE OF BUCKINGHAM
HIS GRACE, LO. HIGH ADMIRALL
OF ENGLAND.

EXCELLENT LO.

S*ALOMON saies: A good Name is as a precious Oyntment; and I assure my selfe such wil your Grace's Name bee with Posteritie. For your Fortune and Merit both have beene Eminent. And you have planted Things that are like to last. I doe now publish my* Essayes; *which, of all my other workes, have beene most Currant: for that, as it seemes, they come home to Men's Businesse and Bosomes. I have enlarged them, both in Number and Weight; so that they are indeed a New Worke. I thought it therefore agreeable to my Affection and Obligation to your Grace, to prefix your Name before them, both in English and in Latine. For I doe conceive, that the Latine Volume of them (being in the Universall Language) may last, as long as Bookes last. My* Instauration, *I dedicated to the King: my* Historie of HENRY the Seventh (*which I have now also translated into Latine*), *and my* Portions *of* Naturall History, *to the Prince: And these I dedicate to your Grace; being of the best Fruits, that by the good Encrease, which God gives to my Pen and Labours, I could yeeld. God leade your Grace by the Hand.*

Your Grace's most obliged and faithfull Servant,

FR. ST. ALBAN.

❧ Of Truth.

WHAT *is Truth?* said jesting Pilate; & would not stay for an answer. Certainly there be that delight in giddinesse, and count it a bondage to fix a beleefe; affecting free-will in thinking, as well as in acting. And though the sects of philosophers of that kinde be gone, yet there remaine certaine discoursing wits, which are of the same veines, though there be not so much bloud in them as was in those of the ancients. But it is not onely the difficultie and labour which men take in finding out of Truth; nor againe, that when it is found, it imposeth upon men's thoughts, that doth bring Lies in favour: but a naturall though corrupt Love of the Lie itselfe. One of the later schoole of the Grecians examineth the matter and is at a stand to thinke what should be in it, that men should love Lies, where neither they make for pleasure, as with poets, nor for advantage, as with the merchant; but for the Lie's sake. But I cannot tell; this same Truth is a naked and open day light, that doth not shew the masques & mummeries and triumphs of the world, halfe so stately and daintily as candle-lights. Truth may perhaps come to the price of a pearle, that sheweth best by day: but it will not rise to the price of a diamond or carbuncle, that sheweth best in varied lights. A mixture of a Lie doth ever adde pleasure. Doth any man doubt, that if there were taken out of men's mindes, vaine opinions, flattering hopes, false valuations, imaginations as one would, and the like, but it would leave the mindes of a number of men poore shrunken things, full of melancholy and indisposition, and unpleasing to themselves? One of the Fathers, in great severity, called poesie, *Vinum dæmonum*, because it filleth the imagination; and yet it is but with the shadow of a Lie. But it is not the Lie that passeth through the minde, but the Lie that sinketh in and setleth in it, that doth the hurt; such as we spake of before. But howsoever these things are thus in men's depraved judgements and affections, yet Truth, which onely doth judge it selfe, teacheth that the inquirie of Truth, which is the love-making, or wooing of it, the knowledge of Truth, which is the presence of it, and the beleefe of Truth, which is the enjoying of it, is the soveraigne good of humane nature. The first creature of God, in the workes of the Dayes, was the light of the sense; the last, was the light of reason; and his Sabbath worke, ever since, is the illumination of his Spirit. First he breathed light upon the face of the matter or chaos; then he breathed light into the face of man; and still he breatheth and inspireth light into the face of his chosen. The poet that beautified the sect that was otherwise inferiour to the rest, saith yet excellently well: *It is a pleasure to stand upon the shore, and to see ships tost upon the Sea: a pleasure to stand in the window of a Castle and to see a Battaile and the Adventures thereof below: But no pleasure is comparable to the standing upon the vantage ground of Truth* (a hill not to be commanded, and where the ayre is alwaies cleare and serene) *and to see the Errours and Wandrings and Mists and Tempests, in the vale below;* so alwaies, that this prospect be with pitty, and not with swelling or pride. Certainly, it is heaven upon earth to have a man's minde move in charitie, rest in providence, and turne upon the poles of Truth.

To passe from theologicall and philosophicall Truth to the Truth of civill businesse; it will be acknowledged, even by those that practize it not, that cleare and round dealing is the honour of man's nature; and that mixture of falshood is like allay in coyne of gold and silver, which may make the metall worke the better, but it embaseth it. For these winding and crooked courses are the goings of the serpent; which goeth basely upon the belly, and not upon the feet. There is no vice that doth so cover a man with shame as to be found false and perfidious. And therefore Mountaigny saith prettily, when he enquired the reason, why the word of the Lie should be such a disgrace and such an odious charge. Saith he, *If it be well weighed, to say that a man lieth is as much to say as that he is brave towards God and a Coward towards Men.* For a Lie faces God, and shrinkes from man. Surely the wickednesse of falshood and breach of faith cannot possibly be so highly expressed as in that it shall be the last peale to call the judgements of God upon the generations of men; it being foretold, that when Christ commeth, *He shall not finde Faith upon the Earth.*

❧ Of Death.

MEN feare Death, as children feare to goe in the darke: and as that natural feare in children is increased with tales, so is the other. Certainly, the contemplation of Death, as the *wages of sinne*, and passage to another world, is holy and religious; but the feare of it, as a tribute due unto nature, is weake. Yet in religious meditations there is sometimes mixture of vanitie & of superstition. You shal reade, in some of the Friars' Books of Mortification, that a man should thinke with himselfe what the paine is, if he have but his fingers end pressed or tortured, and thereby imagine, what the paines of Death are, when the whole body is corrupted and dissolved; when many times Death passeth with lesse paine then the torture of a limme: for the most vitall parts are not the quickest of sense. And by him that spake onely as a philosopher and naturall man, it was well said; *Pompa Mortis magis terret, quam Mors ipsa.* Groanes and convulsions, and a discoloured face, and friends weeping, and blackes, and obsequies, and the like, shew Death terrible. It is worthy the observing, that there is no passion in the minde of man so weake, but it mates and masters the feare of Death; and therefore Death is no such terrible enemie when a man hath so many attendants about him that can winne the combat of him. Revenge triumphs over Death; Love slights it; Honour aspireth to it; Griefe flieth to it; Feare pre-occupateth it; nay we reade, after Otho the Emperour had slaine himselfe, Pitty (which is the tenderest of affections) provoked many to die, out of meere compassion to their soveraigne, and as the truest sort of followers. Nay

Seneca addes nicenesse & satiety; *Cogita quam diu eadem feceris; mori velle, non tantum fortis aut miser, sed etiam fastidiosus potest.* A man would die, though he were neither valiant nor miserable, onely upon a wearinesse to doe the same thing so oft over and over. It is no lesse worthy to observe, how little alteration in good spirits the approaches of Death make; for they appeare to be the same men till the last instant. Augustus Cæsar died in a complement; *Livia, conjugii nostri memor, vive & vale.* Tiberius in dissimulation; as Tacitus saith of him; *Jam Tiberium vires & corpus, non dissimulatio, deserebant.* Vespasian in a jest, sitting upon the stoole; *Ut puto deus fio.* Galba with a sentence; *Feri, si ex re sit populi Romani;* holding forth his necke. Septimius Severus in dispatch; *Adeste, si quid mihi restat agendum.* And the like. Certainly, the Stoikes bestowed too much cost upon Death, and by their great preparations, made it appeare more fearefull. Better saith he, *qui finem vitæ extremum inter munera ponat naturæ.* It is as naturall to die, as to be borne; And to a little infant, perhaps, the one is as painfull as the other. He that dies in an earnest pursuit, is like one that is wounded in hot bloud; who, for the time, scarce feeles the hurt; and therefore, a minde fixt and bent upon somewhat that is good, doth avert the dolors of Death. But above all, beleeve it, the sweetest canticle is, *Nunc dimittis;* when a man hath obtained worthy ends and expectations. Death hath this also; that it openeth the gate to good fame, and extinguisheth envie. *Extinctus amabitur idem.*

❧ Of Unity in Religion.

RELIGION being the chiefe band of humane Society, it is a happy thing when it selfe is well contained within the true band of unity. The quarrels and divisions about Religion were evils unknowne to the heathen. The reason was because the Religion of the heathen consisted rather in rites and ceremonies then in any constant beleefe. For you may imagine what kinde of faith theirs was, when the chiefe Doctors & Fathers of their Church were the poets. But the true God hath this attribute, that he is a *jealous God;* and therefore, his worship and Religion, will endure no mixture nor partner. We shall therefore speake a few words concerning the Unity of the Church; *What are the Fruits thereof; what the Bounds; and what the Meanes?*

The Fruits of Unity (next unto the well pleasing of God, which is all in all) are two: the one, towards those that are without the Church; the other, towards those that are within. For the former; it is certaine that heresies and schismes are of all others, the greatest scandals; yea more then corruption of manners. For as in the naturall body a wound or solution of continuity is worse then a corrupt humor; so in the spirituall. So that nothing doth so much keepe men out of the Church, and drive men out of the Church, as breach of unity. And therefore, whensoever it commeth to that passe, that one saith, *Ecce in deserto,* another saith, *Ecce in penetralibus;* that is, when some men seeke Christ in the conventicles of heretikes and others in an outward face of a Church, that voice had need continually to sound in men's eares, *Nolite exire, goe not out.* The Doctor of the Gentiles (the propriety of whose vocation drew him to have a speciall care of those without) saith, *If an heathen come in, and heare you speake with severall tongues, will he not say that you are mad?* And certainly it is little better, when atheists and prophane persons do heare of so many discordant and contrary opinions in religion; it doth avert them from the Church, and maketh them, *to sit downe in the chaire of the scorners.* It is but a light thing to be vouched in so serious a matter, but yet it expresseth well the deformity. There is a master of scoffing, that in his catalogue of books, of a faigned library, sets downe this title of a booke, *The Morris Daunce of Heretikes.* For indeed every sect of them hath a divers posture, or cringe by themselves, which cannot but move derision in worldlings and depraved politickes, who are apt to contemne holy things.

As for the *Fruit towards those that are within;* it is Peace; which containeth infinite blessings. It establisheth faith; it kindleth charity; the outward peace of the Church distilleth into peace of conscience; and it turneth the labours of writing and reading of controversies into treaties of mortification and devotion.

Concerning the Bounds of Unity; the true placing of them importeth exceedingly. There appeare to be two extremes. For to certaine zelants all speech of pacification is odious. *Is it peace, Jehu? What hast thou to doe with peace? turne thee behinde me.* Peace is not the matter, but following and party. Contrariwise, certaine Laodiceans, and luke-warme persons, thinke they may accommodate points of religion by middle waies, and taking part of both, and witty reconcilements; as if they would make an arbitrement between God and man. Both these extremes are to be avoyded; which will be done, if the league of Christians, penned by our Saviour himselfe, were in the two crosse clauses thereof soundly and plainly expounded; *He that is not with us, is against us:* and againe; *He that is not against us, is with us:* That is, if the points fundamentall and of substance in Religion were truly discerned and distinguished from points not meerely of faith, but of opinion, order, or good intention. This is a thing may seeme to many a matter triviall, and done already: but if it were done lesse partially, it would be embraced more generally.

Of this I may give onely this advice, according to my small modell. Men ought to take heede, of rending God's Church by two kinds of controversies. The one is, when the matter of the point controverted is too small and light, not worth the heat and strife about it, kindled onely by contradiction. For, as it is noted by one of the fathers; *Christs coat, indeed, had no seame: but the Churche's vesture was of divers colours;* whereupon he saith, *In veste varietas sit, scissura non sit;* they be two things, unity and uniformity. The other is, when the matter of the point controverted is great, but it is driven to an over-great subtilty and obscurity; so that it becommeth a thing rather ingenious then substantiall. A man that is of judgement and understanding shall sometimes heare ignorant men differ, and know well within himselfe that those which so differ meane one thing, and yet they themselves would never agree. And if it come to passe, in that distance of judgement, which is betweene man and man, shall wee not thinke that God above, that knowes the heart, doth not discerne that fraile men, in some of their contradictions, intend the same thing; & accepteth of both? The nature of such controversies is excellently expressed by St. Paul in the warning & precept that he giveth concerning the same, *Devita profanas vocum novitates, & oppositiones falsi nominis scientiæ.* Men create oppositions, which are not; and put them into new termes so fixed as whereas the meaning ought to governe the terme, the terme in effect governeth the meaning. There be also two false peaces, or unities; the one, when the peace is grounded but upon an implicite ignorance; for all colours will agree in the darke: the other, when it is peeced up, upon a direct admission of contraries in fundamentall points. For truth and falshood, in such things, are like the Iron and Clay in the toes of Nabucadnezar's image, they may cleave, but they will not incorporate.

Concerning the meanes of procuring Unity; men must beware, that in the procuring or muniting of Religious Unity they doe not dissolve and deface the lawes of charity and of humane society. There be two swords amongst Christians, the spirituall and temporall; and both have their due office and place in the maintenance of Religion. But we may not take up the third sword, which is Mahomets sword, or like unto it! that is, to propagate Religion, by warrs, or by sanguinary persecutions to force consciences; except it be in cases of overt scandall, blasphemy, or intermixture of practize against the state; much lesse to nourish seditions; to authorize conspiracies and rebellions; to put the sword into the peoples' hands; and the like; tending to the subversion of all government, which is the ordinance of God. For this is but to dash the first table against the second; and so to consider men as Christians, as we forget that they are men. Lucretius the poet, when he beheld the act of Agamemnon, that could endure the sacrificing of his owne daughter, exclaimed;

Tantum Relligio potuit suadere malorum.

What would he have said, if he had knowne of the massacre in France, or the powder treason of England? He would have beene seven times more Epicure and Atheist then he was. For as the temporall sword is to bee drawne with great circumspection in cases of Religion; so it is a thing monstrous, to put it into the hands of the common people. Let that bee left unto the Anabaptists, and other furies. It was great blasphemy when the Devill said; *I will ascend, and be like the Highest;* but it is greater blasphemy, to personate God, and bring him in saying; *I will descend, and be like the Prince of Darknesse;* and what is it better, to make the cause of Religion to descend to the cruell and execrable actions, of murthering Princes, butchery of people, and subversion of States and Governments? Surely, this is to bring downe the Holy Ghost, in stead of the likenesse of a dove, in the shape of a vulture, or raven; and to set, out of the barke of a Christian Church, a flagge of a barque of pirats and assassins. Therfore it is most necessary, that the Church by doctrine and decree, Princes by their sword, and all learnings, both Christian and morall, as by their Mercury rod, doe damne and send to hell, for ever, those facts and opinions tending to the support of the same; as hath beene already in good part done. Surely in counsels concerning Religion, that counsel of the Apostle would be prefixed; *Ira hominis non implet Justiciam Dei.* And it was a notable observation, of a wise Father, and no lesse ingenuously confessed; *That those which held and perswaded pressure of consciences, were commonly interested therin, themselves, for their owne ends.*

❧ Of Revenge.

REVENGE is a kinde of wilde justice; which the more man's nature runs to, the more ought law to weed it out. For as for the first wrong, it doth but offend the law; but the revenge of that wrong putteth the law out of office. Certainly, in taking Revenge, a man is but even with his enemy; but in passing it over, he is superiour: for it is a Prince's part to pardon. And Salomon, I am sure, saith; *It is the glory of a man to passe by an offence.* That which is past is gone, and irrevocable; and wise men have enough to doe, with things present and to come; therefore, they doe but trifle with themselves, that labour in past matters. There is no man doth a wrong for the wrong's sake; but therby to purchase himselfe profit, or pleasure, or honour, or the like. Therfore why should I be angry with a man for loving himselfe better than mee? And if any man should doe wrong meerely out of ill nature, why, yet it is but like the thorn, or bryar, which prick and scratch, because they can doe no other. The most tolerable sort of Revenge is for those wrongs which there is no law to remedy: but then, let a man take heed the Revenge be such as there is no law to punish: else a man's enemy is still before hand, and it is two for one. Some, when they take Revenge, are desirous the party should know whence it commeth. This is the more generous. For the delight seemeth to be not so much in doing the hurt as in making the party repent. But base and crafty cowards are like the arrow that flyeth in the darke. Cosmus, duke of Florence, had a desperate saying against perfidious or neglecting friends, as if those wrongs were unpardonable: *You shall reade* (saith he) *that we are commanded to forgive our enemies; but you never read that wee are commanded to forgive our friends.* But yet the spirit of Job was in a better tune; *Shall wee* (saith he) *take good at God's hands, and not be content to take evill also?* And so of friends in a proportion. This is certaine; that a man that studieth Revenge keepes his owne wounds greene, which otherwise would heale and doe well. Publique Revenges are for the most part fortunate; as that for the death of Cæsar; for the death of Pertinax; for the death of Henry the Third of France; and many more. But in Private Revenges it is not so. Nay, rather, vindicative persons live the life of witches; who as they are mischievous, so end they infortunate.

❧ Of Adversity.

IT was an high speech of Seneca, (after the manner of the Stoickes) *that the good things which belong to Prosperity are to be wished; but the good things that belong to Adversity are to be admired. Bona Rerum secundarum optabilia; Adversarum mirabilia.* Certainly if miracles be the command over nature, they appeare most in Adversity. It is yet a higher speech of his then the other, (much too high for a heathen) *It is true greatnesse, to have in one, the frailty of a man, and the security of a God. Vere magnum, habere fragilitatem hominis, securitatem Dei.* This would have done better in Poesy, where transcendences are more allowed. And the poets indeed have beene busy with it; for it is, in effect, the thing which is figured in that strange fiction of the ancient poets, which seemeth not to be without mystery; nay, and to have some approach to the state of a Christian: That *Hercules, when hee went to unbinde Prometheus,* (by whom humane nature is represented) *sailed the length of the great ocean in an earthen pot, or pitcher:* lively describing Christian resolution, that saileth, in the fraile barke of the flesh, thorow the waves of the world. But to speake in a meane. The vertue of Prosperitie, is Temperance; the vertue of Adversity, is Fortitude; which in morals is the more heroicall vertue. Prosperity is the blessing of the Old Testament; Adversity is the blessing of the New; which carrieth the greater benediction, and the clearer revelation of God's favour. Yet, even in the Old Testament, if you listen to David's harpe, you shall heare as many herselike ayres as carols: and the pencill of the Holy Ghost hath laboured more, in describing the afflictions of Job, then the felicities of Salomon. Prosperity is not without many feares and distastes; And Adversity is not without comforts and hopes. Wee see in needle-workes and imbroideries, it is more pleasing to have a lively worke upon a sad and solemne ground, then to have a darke and melancholy worke upon a lightsome ground. Judge therfore of the pleasure of the Heart by the pleasure of the Eye. Certainly, Vertue is like pretious odours, most fragrant when they are incensed or crushed: for Prosperity doth best discover Vice; but Adversity doth best discover Vertue.

Of Simulation and Dissimulation.

DISSIMULATION is but a faint kind of Policy or Wisdome; for it asketh a strong wit and a strong heart to know when to tell truth, & to doe it. Therfore it is the weaker sort of politicks that are the great Dissemblers.

Tacitus saith: *Livia sorted well with the arts of her husband, & dissimulation of her sonne:* attributing arts or policy to Augustus, & dissimulation to Tiberius. And againe, when Mucianus encourageth Vespasian to take arms against Vitellius, he saith: *We rise not against the piercing judgment of Augustus; nor the extreme caution or closenesse of Tiberius.* These properties, of Arts or Policy, and Dissimulation or Closenesse, are indeed habits and faculties severall, and to be distinguished. For if a man have that penetration of judgment as he can discerne what things are to be laid open, and what to be secretted, and what to be shewed at halfe lights, and to whom, and when, (which indeed are arts of State, and arts of Life, as Tacitus well calleth them); to him, a habit of Dissimulation is a hindrance and a poorenesse. But if a man cannot obtaine to that judgment, then it is left to him, generally, to be close, and a Dissembler. For where a man cannot choose or vary in particulars, there it is good to take the safest and wariest way in generall; like the going softly by one that cannot well see. Certainly the ablest men that ever were have had all an opennesse and francknesse of dealing; and a name of certainty and veracity; but then they were like horses well mannaged; for they could tell passing well when to stop or turne: and at such times when they thought the case indeed required Dissimulation, if then they used it, it came to passe that the former opinion spred abroad of their good faith and clearnesse of dealing made them almost invisible.

There be three degrees of this hiding and vailing of a man's selfe. The first Closenesse, Reservation, and Secrecy; when a man leaveth himselfe without observation, or without hold to be taken, what he is. The second, Dissimulation, in the negative; when a man lets fall signes and arguments, that he is not that he is. And the third Simulation, in the affirmative; when a man industriously and expressly faigns, and pretends to be that he is not.

For the first of these, Secrecy; it is indeed, the vertue of a Confessour. And assuredly, the secret man, heareth many Confessions. For who will open himselfe to a blab or a babler? But if a man be thought secret, it inviteth discoverie; as the more close aire sucketh in the more open: and as in confession the revealing is not for worldly use, but for the ease of a man's heart, so secret men come to the knowledge of many things in that kinde; while men rather discharge their mindes then impart their mindes. In few words, mysteries are due to secrecy. Besides (to say truth) nakednesse is uncomely, as well in minde as body; and it addeth no small reverence to men's manners, and actions, if they be not altogether open. As for talkers and futile persons, they are commonly vaine, and credulous withall. For he that talketh what he knoweth, will also talke what he knoweth not. Therfore set it downe; *that an habit of Secrecy is both politick and morall*. And in this part it is good that a man's face give his tongue leave to speake. For the discovery of a man's selfe by the tracts of his countenance is a great weaknesse and betraying; by how much it is many times more marked and beleeved then a man's words.

For the second, which is Dissimulation. It followeth many times upon Secrecy by a necessity: so that he that will be secret must be a Dissembler in some degree. For men are too cunning to suffer a man to keepe an indifferent carriage betweene both, and to be secret, without swaying the ballance on either side. They will so beset a man with questions, and draw him on, and picke it out of him, that without an absurd silence, he must shew an inclination one way; or if he doe not, they will gather as much by his silence as by his speech. As for equivocations, or oraculous speeches, they cannot hold out long. So that no man can be secret, except he give himselfe a little scope of Dissimulation; which is, as it were, but the skirts or traine of Secrecy.

But for the third degree, which is Simulation and false profession; that I hold more culpable, and lesse politicke; except it be in great and rare matters. And therefore a generall custome of Simulation (which is this last degree) is a vice, rising either of a naturall falsenesse or fearefulnesse, or of a minde that hath some maine faults; which because a man must needs disguise, it maketh him practise Simulation in other things lest his hand should be out of use.

The great advantages of Simulation and Dissimulation are three. First, to lay asleepe opposition, and to surprize. For where a man's intentions are published, it is an alarum to call up all that are against them. The second is, to reserve to a man's selfe, a faire retreat. For if a man engage himselfe by a manifest declaration, he must goe through or take a fall. The third is, the better to discover the minde of another. For to him that opens himselfe men will hardly shew themselves adverse; but will (faire) let him goe on, and turne their freedome of speech to freedome of thought. And therefore it is a good shrewd proverbe of the Spaniard; *Tell a lye, and finde a troth.* As if there were no way of discovery, but by Simulation. There be also three disadvantages, to set it even. The first, that Simulation and Dissimulation commonly carry with them a shew of fearfulnesse, which in any businesse doth spoile the feathers of round flying up to the mark. The second, that it pusleth and perplexeth the conceits of many, that perhaps would otherwise co-operate with him; and makes a man walke almost alone to his owne ends. The third and greatest is, that it depriveth a man of one of the most principall instruments for action; which is trust and beleefe. The best composition and temperature is to have Opennesse in fame and opinion; Secrecy in habit; Dissimulation in seasonable use; and a power to faigne, if there be no remedy.

❧ Of Parents and Children.

THE joyes of Parents are secret; and so are their griefes and feares: They cannot utter the one; nor they will not utter the other. Children sweeten labours; but they make misfortunes more bitter: They increase the cares of life; but they mitigate the remembrance of death. The perpetuity by generation is common to beasts; but memory, merit, and noble workes are proper to men: And surely a man shall see the noblest workes and foundations have proceeded from childlesse men; which have sought to expresse the images of their minds, where those of their bodies have failed. So the care of posterity is most in them that have no posterity. They that are the first raisers of their houses are most indulgent towards their Children; beholding them as the continuance not only of their kinde, but of their worke; and so both Children and creatures.

The difference in affection of Parents towards their severall Children is many times unequall; and sometimes unworthy; especially in the mother; as Salomon saith; *A wise sonne rejoyceth the father; but an ungracious sonne shames the mother.* A man shall see, where there is a house full of Children, one or two of the eldest respected, and the youngest made wantons; but in the middest, some that are as it were forgotten, who many times neverthelesse prove the best. The illiberalitie of Parents in allowance towards their Children is an harmefull errour; makes them base; acquaints them with shifts; makes them sort with meane company; and makes them surfet more when they come to plenty. And therefore, the proofe is best, when men keepe their authority towards their Children, but not their purse. Men have a foolish manner (both Parents and schoolemasters and servants) in creating and breeding an emulation between brothers during Childhood, which many times sorteth to discord when they are men, and disturbeth families. The Italians make little difference betweene Children and nephewes, or neere kinsfolkes; but so they be of the lumpe, they care not, though they passe not through their owne body. And, to say truth, in Nature it is much a like matter; in so much, that we see a nephew sometimes resembleth an uncle or a kinsman more then his owne parent; as the bloud happens. Let Parents choose betimes the vocations and courses they meane their Children should take; for then they are most flexible: and let them not too much apply themselves to the disposition of their Children, as thinking they will take best to that which they have most minde to. It is true, that if the affection or aptnesse of the Children be extraordinary, then it is good not to crosse it; but generally the precept is good; *Optimum elige, suave et facile illud faciet consuetudo.* Younger brothers are commonly fortunate, but seldome or never where the elder are disinherited.

❧ Of Marriage and Single Life.

HE that hath wife and children hath given hostages to fortune; for they are impediments to great enterprises, either of vertue or mischiefe. Certainly the best workes, and of greatest merit for the publike, have proceeded from the unmarried or childlesse men; which, both in affection and meanes, have married and endowed the Publike. Yet it were great reason that those that have children should have greatest care of future times; unto which they know they must transmit their dearest pledges. Some there are, who though they lead a single life, yet their thoughts doe end with themselves, and account future times impertinences. Nay, there are some other that account wife and children but as bills of charges. Nay more, there are some foolish rich covetous men, that take a pride in having no children, because they may be thought so much the richer. For perhaps they have heard some talke; *Such an one is a great rich man;* And another except to it; *Yea, but he hath a great charge of children:* as if it were an abatement to his riches. But the most ordinary cause of a single life is liberty; especially in certaine selfe-pleasing and humorous mindes, which are so sensible of every restraint, as they will goe neare to thinke their girdles and garters to be bonds and shackles. Unmarried men are best friends, best masters, best servants; but not alwayes best subjects; for they are light to runne away; and almost all fugitives are of that condition. A single life doth well with Church men: for charity will hardly water the ground, where it must first fill a poole. It is indifferent for judges and magistrates: for if they be facile and corrupt, you shall have a servant five times worse than a wife. For souldiers, I finde the generalls commonly in their hortatives put men in minde of their wives and children: And I thinke the despising of marriage amongst the Turkes maketh the vulgar souldier more base. Certainly wife and children are a kinde of discipline of humanity: and single men, though they be many times more charitable, because their meanes are lesse exhaust, yet, on the other side, they are more cruell and hard hearted, (good to make severe inquisitors) because their tendernesse is not so oft called upon. Grave natures, led by custome, and therfore constant, are commonly loving husbands; as was said of Ulysses; *Vetulam suam præ tulit immortalitati.* Chast women are often proud and froward, as presuming upon the merit of their chastity. It is one of the best bonds both of chastity and obedience in the wife, if she thinke her husband wise; which she will never doe if she finde him jealous. Wives are young men's mistresses; companions for middle age; and old men's nurses. So as a man may have a quarrell to marry when he will. But yet, he was reputed one of the wise men, that made answer to the question: When a man should marry? *A young man not yet, an elder man not at all.* It is often seene that bad husbands have very good wives; whether it be that it rayseth the price of their husband's kindnesse when it comes; or that the wives take a pride in their patience. But this never failes, if the bad husbands were of their owne choosing, against their friends' consent; for then they will be sure to make good their owne folly.

❧ Of Envy.

THERE be none of the affections, which have beene noted to fascinate or bewitch, but Love and Envy. They both have vehement wishes; they frame themselves readily into imaginations, and suggestions; and they come easily into the eye, especially upon the presence of the objects; which are the points that conduce to fascination, if any such thing there be. We see likewise the Scripture calleth Envy an *evill eye:* and the astrologers call the evill influences of the starrs *evill aspects;* so that still there seemeth to be acknowledged, in the act of Envy, an ejaculation or irradiation of the eye. Nay, some have beene so curious as to note that the times when the stroke or percussion of an envious eye doth most hurt, are when the party envied is beheld in glory or triumph; for that sets an edge upon Envy; and besides, at such times the spirits of the person envied doe come forth, most into the outward parts, and so meet the blow.

But leaving these Curiosities, (though not unworthy, to be thought on in fit place) wee will handle, *what persons are apt to envy others; what persons are most subject to be envied themselves;* and, *what is the difference between publique and private Envy.*

A man that hath no vertue in himselfe, ever envieth vertue in others. For men's mindes will either feed upon their owne good or upon other's evill; and who wanteth the one will prey upon the other; and who so is out of hope to attaine to another's vertue, will seeke to come at even hand, by depressing an other's fortune.

A man that is busy and inquisitive is commonly envious. For to know much of other men's matters cannot be because all that adoe may concerne his own estate; therfore it must needs be that he taketh a kinde of plaie-pleasure in looking upon the fortunes of others. Neither can he that mindeth but his own businesse finde much matter for Envy. For Envy is a gadding passion, and walketh the streets, and doth not keepe home; *Non est curiosus, quin idem sit malevolus.*

Men of noble birth are noted to be envious towards new men when they rise. For the distance is altered, and it is like a deceipt of the eye, that when others come on they thinke themselves goe backe.

Deformed persons, and eunuches, and old men, and bastards, are envious. For he that cannot possibly mend his owne case will doe what he can to impaire anothers; except these defects light upon a very brave and heroicall nature, which thinketh to make his naturall wants part of his honour; in that it should be said, that an eunuch, or a lame man, did such great matters; affecting the honour of a miracle; as it was in Narses the eunuch, and Agesilaus and Tamberlanes, that were lame men.

The same is the case of men that rise after calamities and misfortunes; for they are as men fallen out with the times; and thinke other men's harmes a redemption of their owne sufferings.

They that desire to excell in too many matters, out of levity and vaine glory, are ever envious. For they cannot want worke; it being impossible, but many in some one of those things, should surpasse them. Which was the character of Adrian the Emperour, that mortally envied poets and painters and artificers, in works wherein he had a veine to excell.

Lastly, neare kinsfolks, and fellowes in office, and those that have beene bred together, are more apt to envy their equals when they are raised. For it doth upbraid unto them their owne fortunes, and pointeth at them, and commeth oftner into their remembrance, and incurreth likewise more into the note of others: and Envy ever redoubleth from speech and fame. Cain's Envy was the more vile and malignant towards his brother Abel because, when his sacrifice was better accepted, there was no body to looke on. Thus much for *those that are apt to Envy.*

Concerning *those that are more or lesse subject to Envy:* First, persons of eminent vertue, when they are advanced, are lesse envied. For their fortune seemeth but due unto them; and no man envieth the payment of a debt, but rewards and liberality rather. Againe, Envy is ever joyned with the comparing of a man's selfe; and where there is no comparison, no Envy; & therefore Kings are not envied but by Kings. Neverthelesse it is to be noted that unworthy persons are most envied at their first comming in, and afterwards overcome it better; whereas contrariwise, persons of worth and merit are most envied when their fortune continueth long. For by that time, though their vertue be the same, yet it hath not the same lustre; for fresh men grow up that darken it.

Persons of Noble Bloud are lesse envied in their rising: For it seemeth but right done to their birth. Besides, there seemeth not much added to their fortune; and Envy is as the sunne beames, that beat hotter upon a bank or steepe rising ground, then upon a flat. And for the same reason those that are advanced by degrees are lesse envied then those that are advanced suddainly and *per saltum.*

Those that have joyned with their honour great travels, cares, or perills, are lesse subject to Envy. For men thinke that they earne their honours hardly, and pitty them sometimes; and pitty ever healeth Envy. Wherefore, you shall observe that the more deepe and sober sort of politique persons, in their greatnesse, are ever bemoaning themselves, what a life they lead; chanting a *quanta patimur*. Not that they feele it so, but onely to abate the edge of Envy. But this is to be understood of businesse that is laid upon men, and not such as they call unto themselves. For nothing increaseth Envy more then an unnecessary and ambitious ingrossing of businesse. And nothing doth extinguish Envy more then for a great person to preserve all other inferiour officers in their full rights and preheminences of their places. For by that meanes there be so many skreenes betweene him and Envy.

Above all, those are most subject to Envy, which carry the greatnesse of their fortunes in an insolent and proud manner: being never well but while they are shewing how great they are, either by outward pompe, or by triumphing over all opposition or competition; whereas wise men will rather doe sacrifice to Envy, in suffering themselves sometimes of purpose to be crost and overborne in things that doe not much concerne them. Notwithstanding, so much is true; that the carriage of greatnesse in a plaine and open manner (so it be without arrogancy and vaine glory) doth draw lesse Envy then if it be in a more crafty and cunning fashion. For in that course, a man doth but disavow fortune; and seemeth to be conscious of his owne want in worth; and doth but teach others to envy him.

Lastly, to conclude this part; as we said in the beginning that the act of Envy had somewhat in it of witchcraft, so there is no other cure of Envy but the cure of witchcraft: and that is, to remove the *lot* (as they call it) and to lay it upon another.

For which purpose, the wiser sort of great persons bring in ever upon the stage some body upon whom to derive the Envie that would come upon themselves; sometimes upon ministers and servants; sometimes upon colleagues and associates; and the like; and for that turne there are never wanting some persons of violent natures, who so they may have power and businesse, will take it at any cost.

Now to speake of publique Envy. There is yet some good in publique Envy; whereas in private there is none. For publique Envy is as an ostracisme, that eclipseth men when they grow too great. And therefore it is a bridle also to great ones, to keepe them within bounds.

This Envy, being in the Latine word *invidia*, goeth in the moderne languages by the name of *discontentment:* of which we shall speake in handling Sedition. It is a disease in a State like to infection. For as infection spreadeth upon that which is sound, and tainteth it; so when Envy is gotten once into a State, it traduceth even the best actions thereof, and turneth them into an ill odour. And therefore there is little won by intermingling of plausible actions. For that doth argue but a weaknesse and feare of Envy, which hurteth so much the more, as it is likewise usuall in infections; which if you feare them, you call them upon you.

This publique Envy seemeth to beat chiefly upon principall Officers or Ministers, rather then upon Kings and Estates themselves. But this is a sure rule, that if the Envy upon the Minister be great, when the cause of it in him is smal; or if the Envy be generall in a manner upon all the Ministers of an Estate; then the Envy (though hidden) is truly upon the State it selfe. And so much of publike Envy or discontentment, and the difference thereof from private Envy, which was handled in the first place.

We will adde this in generall, touching the affection of Envy; that of all other affections, it is the most importune and continuall. For of other affections there is occasion given but now and then: and therefore it was well said, *Invidia festos dies non agit.* For it is ever working upon some or other. And it is also noted that love and Envy doe make a man pine, which other affections doe not; because they are not so continuall. It is also the vilest affection, and the most depraved; for which cause it is the proper attribute of the Devill, who is called *the envious man, that soweth tares amongst the wheat by night.* As it alwayes commeth to passe, that Envy worketh subtilly, and in the darke; and to the prejudice of good things, such as is the wheat.

❧ Of Love.

THE stage is more beholding to Love then the life of man. For as to the stage, Love is ever matter of comedies, and now and then of tragedies: but in life it doth much mischiefe; sometimes like a Syren, sometimes like a Fury. You may observe that amongst all the great and worthy persons (whereof the memory remaineth, either ancient or recent) there is not one that hath beene transported to the mad degree of Love: which shewes that great spirits and great businesse doe keepe out this weake passion. You must except neverthelesse Marcus Antonius, the halfe partner of the empire of Rome; and Appius Claudius, the decemvir and law-giver; whereof the former was indeed a voluptuous man, and inordinate; but the latter was an austere and wise man: and therefore it seemes (though rarely) that Love can finde entrance not only into an open heart, but also into a heart well fortified, if watch be not well kept. It is a poore saying of Epicurus: *Satis magnum alter alteri theatrum sumus:* as if man, made for the contemplation of heaven and all noble objects, should doe nothing but kneele before a little idoll, and make himselfe subject, though not of the mouth (as beasts are), yet of the eye; which was given him for higher purposes. It is a strange thing to note the excesse of this passion, and how it braves the nature and value of things, by this, that the speaking in a perpetuall hyperbole is comely in nothing but in Love. Neither is it meerely in the phrase; for whereas it hath beene well said that the arch-flatterer, with whom all the petty flatterers have intelligence, is a man's selfe; certainly the lover is more. For there was never proud man thought so absurdly well of himselfe as the lover doth of the person loved; and therefore, it was well said; *That it is impossible to love and to be wise.* Neither doth this weaknesse appeare to others onely, and not to the party loved; but to the loved, most of all, except the love be reciproque. For it is a true rule, that love is ever rewarded either with the reciproque or with an inward and secret contempt. By how much the more men ought to beware of this passion, which loseth not only other things, but it selfe. As for the other losses, the poet's relation doth well figure them; that he that preferred Helena, quitted the gifts of Juno, and Pallas. For whosoever esteemeth too much of amorous affection quitteth both riches and wisedome. This passion hath his flouds in the very times of weaknesse; which are great prosperitie and great adversitie; though this latter hath beene less observed: both which times kindle Love and make it more fervent, and therefore shew it to be the childe of folly. They doe best, who if they cannot but admit Love, yet make it keepe quarter: and sever it wholly from their serious affaires and actions of life: for if it checke once with businesse, it troubleth men's fortunes, and maketh men that they can no wayes be true to their owne ends. I know not how, but martiall men are given to love: I thinke it is but as they are given to wine; for perils commonly aske to be paid in pleasures. There is in man's nature a secret inclination and motion towards love of others; which, if it be not spent upon some one or a few, doth naturally spread it selfe towards many, and maketh men become humane and charitable; as it is seene sometime in Friars. Nuptiall Love maketh mankinde; friendly Love perfecteth it; but wanton Love corrupteth & imbaseth it.

❧ Of Great Place.

MEN in Great Place are thrice servants: servants of the Soveraigne or State; servants of Fame; and servants of Businesse. So as they have no freedome; neither in their persons, nor in their actions, nor in their times. It is a strange desire, to seeke power and to lose libertie; or to seeke power over others, and to loose power over a man's selfe. The rising unto Place is laborious; and by paines men come to greater paines; and it is sometimes base; and by indignities men come to dignities. The standing is slippery and the regresse is either a downefall, or at least an eclipse, which is a melancholy thing. *Cum non sis qui fueris, non esse cur velis vivere.* Nay, retire men cannot when they would; neither will they when it were reason; but are impatient of privatenesse, even in age and sicknesse, which require the shadow; like old townesmen, that will be still sitting at their street doore, though thereby they offer age to scorne. Certainly great persons had need to borrow other men's opinions, to thinke themselves happy; for if they judge by their owne feeling, they cannot finde it; but if they thinke with themselves what other men thinke of them, and that other men would faine be as they are, then they are happy as it were by report; when perhaps they finde the contrary within. For they are the first that finde their owne griefs, though they be the last that finde their owne faults. Certainly, men in great fortunes are strangers to themselves, and while they are in the pusle of businesse they have no time to tend their health, either of body or minde. *Illi mors gravis incubat, qui notus nimis omnibus, igno-*

tus moritur sibi. In Place there is license to doe good and evill; wherof the latter is a curse; for in evill the best condition is not to Will; the second, not to Can. But power to doe good is the true and lawfull end of aspiring. For good thoughts (though God accept them) yet towards men are little better then good dreames, except they be put in act; and that cannot be without power, and Place, as the vantage and commanding ground. Merit and good works, is the end of man's motion; and conscience of the same is the accomplishment of man's rest. For if a man, can be partaker of God's theater, he shall likewise be partaker of God's rest. *Et conversus Deus, ut aspiceret opera, quæ fecerunt manus suæ vidit quod omnia essent bona nimis;* and then the Sabbath. In the discharge of thy Place, set before thee the best examples; for imitation is a globe of precepts. And after a time set before thee thine owne example; and examine thy selfe strictly whether thou didst not best at first. Neglect not also the examples of those that have carried themselves ill, in the same Place; not to set off thy selfe by taxing their memory, but to direct thy selfe what to avoid. Reforme therfore, without braverie or scandall of former times and persons; but yet set it downe to thy selfe as well to create good presidents as to follow them. Reduce things to the first institution, and observe wherin and how they have degenerate; but yet aske counsell of both Times; of the Ancient Time, what is best; and of the Latter Time, what is fittest. Seeke to make thy course regular, that men may know before hand what they may expect; but be not too positive and peremptorie; and expresse thy selfe well when thou digressest from thy rule. Preserve the right of thy Place; but stirre not questions of jurisdiction; and rather, assume thy right in silence and *de facto*, then voice it with claimes and challenges. Preserve likewise the rights of inferiour Places; and thinke it more honour to direct in chiefe then to be busie in all. Embrace and invite helps and advices touching the execution of thy Place; and doe not drive away such as bring thee information, as medlers; but accept of them in good part. The vices of authoritie are chiefly foure: Delaies, Corruption, Roughnesse, and Facilitie. For Delaies; give easie accesse; keepe times appointed; goe through with that which is in hand; and interlace not businesse but of necessitie. For Corruption; doe not onely binde thine owne hands or thy servants' hands from taking, but binde the hands of sutours also from offring. For integritie used doth the one; but integritie professed, and with a manifest detestation of bribery, doth the other. And avoid not onely the fault, but the suspicion. Whosoever is found variable, and changeth manifestly without manifest cause, giveth suspicion of Corruption. Therefore, alwayes, when thou changest thine opinion or course, professe it plainly, and declare it, together with the reasons that move thee to change; and doe not thinke to steale it. A servant or a favorite, if hee be inward, and no other apparant cause of esteeme, is commonly thought but a by-way, to close Corruption. For Roughnesse; it is a needlesse cause of discontent: severitie breedeth feare, but Roughnesse breedeth hate. Even reproofes from authoritie ought to be grave, and not taunting. As for Facilitie; it is worse then bribery. For bribes come but now and then; but if importunitie or idle respects lead a man, he shall never be without. As Salomon saith; *to respect persons is not good; for such a man will transgresse for a peece of bread.* It is most true, that was anciently spoken; *a place sheweth the man.* And it sheweth some to the better, and some to the worse. *Omnium consensu, capax imperii, nisi imperasset;* saith Tacitus of Galba: but of Vespasian he saith; *Solus imperan-*

tium Vespasianus mutatus in melius. Though the one was meant of sufficiencie, the other of manners and affection. It is an assured signe of a worthy and generous spirit, whom honour amends. For honour is, or should be, the Place of vertue: and as in Nature things move violently to their Place and calmely in their Place; so vertue in ambition is violent, in authoritie setled and calme. All rising to Great Place is by a winding staire; and if there be factions, it is good to side a man's selfe whilest hee is in the rising, and to ballance himselfe when hee is placed. Use the memory of thy predecessour fairely and tenderly; for if thou dost not, it is a debt will sure be paid when thou art gone. If thou have colleagues, respect them, and rather call them when they looke not for it, then exclude them when they have reason to looke to be called. Be not too sensible or too remembring of thy Place, in conversation and private answers to suitors; but let it rather be said, *When he sits in Place, he is another man.*

❧ Of Boldnesse.

IT is a triviall grammar schoole text, but yet worthy a wise man's consideration. Question was asked of Demosthenes; *What was the chiefe part of an Oratour?* He answered, Action; what next? Action; what next again? Action. He said it that knew it best; and had by nature himselfe no advantage in that he commended. A strange thing, that that part of an Oratour which is but superficiall, and rather the Vertue of a Player, should be placed so high, above those other noble parts, of invention, elocution, and the rest: nay almost alone, as if it were all in all. But the reason is plaine. There is in humane nature generally more of the foole then of the wise; and therfore those faculties by which the foolish part of men's mindes is taken are most potent. Wonderfull like is the case of Boldnesse in civill businesse; what first? Boldnesse; what second, and third? Boldnesse. And yet Boldnesse is a childe of ignorance and basenesse, farre inferiour to other parts. But neverthelesse it doth fascinate, and binde hand and foot those, that are either shallow in judgment or weake in courage, which are the greatest part; yea and prevaileth with wise men at weake times. Therfore we see it hath done wonders in popular States; but with Senates and Princes lesse; and more ever upon the first entrance of bold persons into action then soone after; for Boldnesse is an ill keeper of promise. Surely as there are mountebanques for the naturall body, so are there mountebanques for the politique body; men that undertake great cures, and perhaps have been lucky in two or three experiments, but want the grounds of science, and therfore cannot hold out. Nay you shall see a bold fellow many times doe Mahomet's miracle. Mahomet made the people beleeve, that he would call an hill to him, and from the top of it offer up his praiers, for the observers of his law. The people assembled; Mahomet cald the hill to come to him, againe and againe; and when the hill stood still, he was never a whit abashed, but said; *If the hill will not come to Mahomet, Mahomet wil go to the hil.* So these men, when they have promised great matters and failed most shamefully, (yet if they have the perfection of Boldnesse) they will but slight it over, and make a turne, and no more adoe. Certainly, to men of great judgment, bold persons are a sport to behold; nay and to the vulgar also, Boldnesse hath somewhat of the ridiculous. For if absurdity be the subject of laughter, doubt you not but great Boldnesse is seldome without some absurdity. Especially, it is a sport to see, when a bold fellow is out of countenance; for that puts his face into a most shruncken & woodden posture; as needes it must; for in bashfulnesse the spirits doe a little goe and come; but with bold men, upon like occasion, they stand at a stay; like a stale at chesse, where it is no mate, but yet the game cannot stirre. But this last were fitter for a satyre then for a serious observation. This is well to be weighed; that Boldnesse is ever blinde; for it seeth not dangers and inconveniences. Therfore it is ill in counsell, good in execution: so that the right use of bold persons is, that they never command in chiefe, but be seconds, and under the direction of others. For in counsell, it is good to see dangers; and in execution not to see them, except they be very great.

❧ Of Goodnesse, and Goodnesse of Nature.

I TAKE Goodnesse in this sense, the affecting of the weale of men, which is that the Grecians call *philanthropia;* & the word *humanitie* (as it is used) is a little too light to expresse it. Goodnesse I call the habit, and Goodnesse of Nature the inclination. This of all vertues, and dignities of the minde is the greatest; being the character of the Deitie: and without it man is a busie, mischievous, wretched thing; no better then a kinde of vermine. Goodnesse answers to the theologicall vertue charitie, and admits no excesse, but errour. The desire of power in excesse caused the angels to fall; the desire of knowledge in excesse caused man to fall; but in charity, there is no excesse; neither can angell or man come in danger by it. The inclination to Goodnesse is imprinted deepely in the nature of man; in so much that if it issue not towards men, it will take unto other living creatures; as it is seen in the Turks, a cruell people, who neverthelesse are kinde to beasts, and give almes to dogs and birds: in so much, as Busbechius reporteth; a Christian boy in Constantinople had like to have been stoned for gagging, in a waggishnesse, a long billed fowle. Errours indeed in this vertue of goodnesse or charity, may be committed. The Italians have an ungracious proverb; *Tanto buon che val niente: so good, that he is good for nothing*. And one of the doctors of Italy, Nicholas Macciavel, had the confidence to put in writing, almost in plaine termes: *That the Christian faith had given up good men in prey to those that are tyrannicall and unjust.* Which he spake, because indeed there was never law or sect or opinion did so much magnifie Goodnesse as the Christian religion doth. Therfore to avoid the scandall and the danger both, it is good to take knowledge of the errours of an habit so excellent. Seeke the good of other men, but be not in bondage to their faces or fancies; for that is but facilitie or softnesse; which taketh an honest minde prisoner. Neither give thou Æsops cocke a gemme, who would be better pleased and happier if he had had a barly corne. The example of God teacheth the lesson truly: *He sendeth his raine, and maketh his sunne to shine, upon the just and unjust;* but hee doth not raine wealth nor shine honour and vertues, upon men equally. Common benefits are to be communicate with all; but peculiar benefits, with choice. And beware, how in making the portraiture, thou breakest the patterne: for Divinitie maketh the love of our selves the patterne; the love of our neighbours but the portraiture. *Sell all thou hast, and give it to the poore, and follow mee:* but sell not all thou hast, except thou come and follow mee; that is, except thou have a vocation wherin thou maist doe as much good with little meanes as with great: for otherwise in feeding the streames thou driest the fountaine. Neither is there only a habit of Goodnesse, directed by right reason; but there is in some men, even in Nature, a disposition towards it: as on the other side there is a naturall malignitie. For there be that in their nature doe not affect the good of others. The lighter sort of malignitie, turneth but to a crosnesse, or frowardnesse, or aptnesse to oppose, or difficilnesse, or the like; but the deeper sort to envy and meere mischiefe. Such men in other men's calamities, are, as it were, in season, and are ever on the loading part; not so good as the dogs that licked Lazarus' sores; but like flies that are still buzzing upon any thing that is raw; *misanthropi*, that make it their practise to bring men to the bough; and yet have never a tree for the purpose in their gardens, as Timon had. Such dispositions, are the very errours of humane nature: and yet they are the fittest timber to make great politiques of: like to knee timber, that is good for ships, that are ordained to be tossed; but not for building houses, that shall stand firme. The parts and signes of Goodnesse are many. If a man be gracious and curteous to strangers, it shewes he is a citizen of the world, and that his heart is no island cut off from other lands, but a continent that joynes to them. If he be compassionate towards the afflictions of others, it shewes that his heart is like the noble tree that is wounded it selfe when it gives the balme. If he easily pardons and remits offences, it shews that his minde is planted above injuries; so that he cannot be shot. If he be thankfull for small benefits, it shewes that he weighes men's mindes, and not their trash. But above all, if he have St. Paul's perfection, that he would wish to be an *anathema* from Christ for the salvation of his brethren, it shewes much of a divine nature, and a kinde of conformity with Christ himselfe.

❧ Of Nobility.

WE will speake of Nobility, first as a portion of an Estate, then as a condition of particular persons. A Monarchy, where there is no Nobility at all, is ever a pure and absolute Tyranny; as that of the Turkes. For Nobility attempers Soveraignty, and drawes the eyes of the people somewhat aside from the line royall. But for democracies, they need it not; and they are commonly more quiet and lesse subject to sedition then where there are stirps of Nobles. For men's eyes are upon the businesse, and not upon the persons: or if upon the persons, it is for the businesse sake, as fittest, and not for flags and pedegree. Wee see the Switzers last well, notwithstanding their diversitie of religion and of cantons. For utility is their bond, and not respects. The united provinces of the Low Countries in their government excell: for where there is an equality, the consultations are more indifferent, and the payments and tributes more cheerfull. A great and potent Nobility addeth majestie to a monarch, but diminisheth power; and putteth life and spirit into the people, but presseth their fortune. It is well when Nobles are not too great for soveraignty nor for justice; and yet maintained in that height, as the insolencie of inferiours may be broken upon them before it come on too fast upon the majesty of kings. A numerous Nobility causeth poverty and inconvenience in a State: for it is a surcharge of expence; and besides, it being of necessity that many of the Nobility fall in time to be weake in fortune, it maketh a kinde of disproportion betweene honour & meanes.

As for Nobility in particular persons; it is a reverend thing to see an ancient castle or building not in decay; or to see a faire timber tree sound and perfect. How much more, to behold an ancient noble family, which hath stood against the waves and weathers of time. For new Nobility is but the act of power; but ancient Nobility is the act of time. Those that are first raised to Nobility are commonly more vertuous, but lesse innocent, then their descendants: for there is rarely any rising but by a commixture of good and evill arts. But it is reason the memory of their vertues remaine to their posterity, and their faults die with themselves. Nobility of birth commonly abateth industry: and he that is not industrious envieth him that is. Besides, Noble persons cannot goe much higher; and he that standeth at a stay, when others rise, can hardly avoid motions of envy. On the other side, Nobility extinguisheth the passive envy from others towards them; because they are in possession of honour. Certainly Kings, that have able men of their Nobility, shall finde ease in imploying them; and a better slide into their businesse: for people naturally bend to them, as borne in some sort to command.

❧ Of Seditions and Troubles.

SHEPHEARDS of people had need know the kalenders of tempests in State; which are commonly greatest, when things grow to equality; as naturall tempests are greatest about the *Æquinoctia*. And as there are certaine hollow blasts of winde and secret swellings of seas before a tempest, so are there in States:

Ille etiam cæcos instare tumultus
Sæpe monet, fraudesque, & operta tumescere bella.

Libels and licentious discourses against the State, when they are frequent and open; and in like sort, false newes often running up and downe to the disadvantage of the State, and hastily embraced; are amongst the signes of troubles. Virgil giving the pedegre of Fame, saith, *she was sister to the giants.*

Illam Terra parens ira irritata Deorum,
Extremam (ut perhibent) Cæo Enceladoque sororem
Progenuit.—

as if Fames were the reliques of Seditions past; but they are no lesse, indeed, the preludes of Seditions to come. Howsoever he noteth it right, that Seditious Tumults, and Seditious Fames differ no more but as brother and sister, masculine and feminine; especially, if it come to that, that the best actions of a State, and the most plausible, and which ought to give greatest contentment, are taken in ill sense, and traduced: for that shewes the envy great, as Tacitus saith; *Conflata magna invidia, seu bene, seu male, gesta premunt.* Neither doth it follow, that because these Fames are a signe of Troubles, that the suppressing of them with too much severity should be a remedy of Troubles. For the despising of them many times checks them best; and the going about to stop them doth but make a wonder long-lived. Also that kinde of obedience which Tacitus speaketh of, is to be held suspected; *Erant in officio, sed tamen qui mallent mandata imperantium interpretari, quam exequi;* disputing, excusing, cavilling upon mandates and directions, is a kinde of shaking off the yoake, and assay of disobedience: especially if in those disputings they which are for the direction speake fearefully and tenderly; and those that are against it, audaciously.

Also, as Macciavel noteth well, when Princes, that ought to be common parents, make themselves as a party, and leane to a side, it is as a boat that is overthrowen by uneven weight on the one side; as was well seen, in the time of Henry the third of France: for first, himselfe entred league for the extirpation of the Protestants; and presently after, the same league was turned upon himselfe. For when the authority of Princes is made but an accessary to a cause, and that there be other bands, that tie faster then the band of soveraignty, Kings begin to be put almost out of possession.

Also, when discords, and quarrells, and factions are carried openly and audaciously; it is a signe the reverence of government is lost. For the motions of the greatest persons in a government ought to be as the motions of the planets under *primum mobile;* (according to the old opinion), which is, that every of them is carried swiftly by the highest motion, and softly in their owne motion. And therfore, when great ones in their owne particular motion move violently, and, as Tacitus expresseth it well, *Liberius, quam ut imperantium meminissent;* it is a signe the orbs are out of frame. For reverence is that wherwith Princes are girt from God; who threatneth the dissolving thereof; *Solvam cingula regum.*

So when any of the foure pillars of government are mainly shaken or weakned (which are Religion, Justice, Counsell, and Treasure), men had need to pray for faire weather. But let us passe from this part of predictions, (concerning which, neverthelesse, more light may be taken from that which followeth); and let us speake first of the materials of Seditions; then of the Motives of them; and thirdly of the Remedies.

Concerning the materialls of Seditions. It is a thing well to be considered; for the surest way to prevent Seditions (if the times doe beare it) is to take away the matter of them. For if there be fuell prepared, it is hard to tell whence the spark shall come that shall set it on fire. The matter of Seditions is of two kindes; much poverty and much discontentment. It is certaine, so many overthrowne estates, so many votes for troubles. Lucan noteth well the State of Rome, before the Civill Warre.

Hinc usura vorax, rapidumque in tempore fænus,
Hinc concussa fides, & multis utile bellum.

This same *multis utile bellum* is an assured and infallible signe of a State, disposed to Seditions, and Troubles. And if this poverty, and broken estate in the better sort, be joyned with a want and necessity in the meane people, the danger is imminent and great. For the rebellions of the belly are the worst. As for Discontentments, they are in the politique body, like to humours in the naturall, which are apt to gather a preternaturall heat & to enflame. And let no prince measure the danger of them, by this; whether they be just, or unjust; for that were to imagine people to be too reasonable; who doe often spurne at their owne good: nor yet by this; whether the griefes wherupon they rise be in fact great or small: for they are the most dangerous Discontentments, where the feare is greater then the feeling. *Dolendi modus, timendi non item.* Besides, in great oppressions, the same things that provoke the patience, doe withall mate the courage: but in feares it is not so. Neither let any Prince or State be secure concerning Discontentments, because they have been often, or have been long, and yet no perill hath ensued; for as it is true that every vapor or fume doth not turne into a storme; so it is neverthelesse true that stormes, though they blow over divers times, yet may fall at last; and as the Spanish proverb noteth well; *The cord breaketh at the last by the weakest pull.*

The causes and motives of Seditions are; innovation in religion; taxes; alteration of lawes and customes; breaking of priviledges; generall oppression; advancement of unworthy persons; strangers; dearths; disbanded souldiers; factions growne desperate; and whatsoever, in offending people, joyneth and knitteth them in a common cause.

For the Remedies; there may be some generall preservatives, whereof wee will speake; as for the just cure, it must answer to the particular disease: and so be left to counsell rather then rule.

The first Remedy or prevention is to remove by all meanes possible that materiall cause of Sedition wherof we spake; which is want and poverty in the estate. To which purpose serveth the opening and well ballancing of trade; the cherishing of manufactures; the banishing of idlenesse; the repressing of waste and excesse by sumptuary lawes; the improvement and husbanding of the soyle; the regulating of prices of things vendible; the moderating of taxes and tributes; and the like. Generally, it is to be foreseene that the population of a Kingdome (especially if it be not mowen downe by warrs) doe not exceed the stock of the kingdome, which should maintaine them. Neither is the population to be reckoned onely by number: for a smaller number that spend more & earne lesse doe weare out an estate sooner then a greater number that live lower & gather more. Therefore the multiplying of Nobilitie and other degrees of qualitie in an over proportion to the common people doth speedily bring a State to necessitie: and so doth likewise an over-growne clergie; for they bring nothing to the stocke; and in like manner, when more are bred schollers then preferments can take off.

It is likewise to be remembred, that for as much as the increase of any estate must be upon the forrainer (for whatsoever is some where gotten is some where lost) there be but three things which one nation selleth unto another; the commoditie as nature yeeldeth it; the manufacture; and the vecture or carriage. So that if these three wheeles goe, wealth will flow as in a spring tide. And it commeth many times to passe that *materiam superabit opus;* that the worke and carriage is more worth then the materiall, and enricheth a State more; as is notably seene in the Low-Countrey-men, who have the best mines above ground in the world.

Above all things, good policie is to be used that the treasure and moneyes in a State be not gathered into few hands. For otherwise a State may have a great stock, and yet starve. And money is like muck, not good except it be spread. This is done chiefly by suppressing or at the least keeping a strait hand upon the devouring trades of usurie, ingrossing, great pasturages, and the like.

For removing discontentments, or at least the danger of them; there is in every State (as we know) two portions of subjects; the Noblesse and the Commonaltie. When one of these is discontent, the danger is not great; for common people are of slow motion, if they be not excited by the greater sort; and the greater sort are of small strength, except the multitude be apt and ready to move of themselves. Then is the danger, when the greater sort doe but wait for the troubling of the waters amongst the meaner, that then they may declare themselves. The poets faigne that the rest of the gods, would have bound Jupiter; which he hearing of, by the counsell of Pallas, sent for Briareus, with his hundred hands, to come in to his aid. An embleme, no doubt, to shew how safe it is for Monarchs, to make sure of the good will of common people.

To give moderate liberty for griefes and discontentments to evaporate (so it be without too great insolency or bravery), is a safe way. For he that turneth the humors backe, and maketh the wound bleed inwards, endangereth maligne ulcers and pernicious impostumations.

The part of Epimetheus mought well become Prometheus in the case of discontentments; for there is not a better provision against them. Epimetheus, when griefes and evils flew abroad, at last shut the lid, and kept hope in the bottome of the vessell. Certainly, the politique and artificiall nourishing and entertaining of hopes, and carrying men from hopes to hopes, is one of the best antidotes against the poyson of discontentments. And it is a certaine signe of a wise government and proceeding, when it can hold men's hearts by hopes, when it cannot by satisfaction: and when it can handle things in such manner, as no evill shall appeare so peremptory but that it hath some out-let of hope: which is the lesse hard to doe, because both particular persons and factions are apt enough to flatter themselves, or at least to brave that which they beleeve not.

Also the foresight and prevention that there be no likely or fit head whereunto discontented persons may resort, and under whom they may joyne, is a knowne, but an excellent point of caution. I understand a fit head to be one that hath greatnesse & reputation; that hath confidence with the discontented party, and upon whom they turne their eyes; and that is thought discontented in his own particular; which kinde of persons are either to be wonne and reconciled to the State, and that in a fast and true manner; or to be fronted with some other of the same party, that may oppose them, and so divide the reputation. Generally, the dividing and breaking of all factions and combinations that are adverse to the State, and setting them at distance, or at least distrust amongst themselves, is not one of the worst remedies. For it is a desperate case, if those that hold with the proceeding of the State be full of discord and faction; and those that are against it be entire and united.

I have noted that some witty and sharpe speeches which have fallen from Princes have given fire to Seditions. Cæsar did himselfe infinite hurt in that speech, *Sylla nescivit literas, non potuit dictare:* for it did utterly cut off that hope which men had entertained, that he would at one time or other give over his dictatorship. Galba undid himselfe by that speech, *Legi à se militem, non emi:* for it put the souldiers out of hope of the donative. Probus likewise, by that speech, *Si vixero, non opus erit amplius Romano imperio militibus;* a speech of great despaire for the souldiers. And many the like. Surely Princes had need, in tender matters and ticklish times, to beware what they say; especially in these short speeches, which flie abroad like darts, and are thought to be shot out of their secret intentions. For as for large discourses, they are flat things, and not so much noted.

Lastly, let Princes, against all events, not be without some great person, one or rather more, of military valour neere unto them, for the repressing of Seditions, in their beginnings. For without that, there useth to be more trepidation in court, upon the first breaking out of troubles, then were fit. And the State runneth the danger of that which Tacitus saith; *Atque is habitus animorum fuit, ut pessimum facinus auderent pauci, plures vellent, omnes paterentur.* But let such military persons be assured, and well reputed of, rather then factious & popular; holding also good correspondence with the other great men in the State; or else the remedie is worse then the disease.

❧ Of Atheisme.

I HAD rather beleeve all the fables in the Legend, and the Talmud, and the Alcoran, then that this universall frame is without a minde. And therefore God never wrought miracle, to convince Atheisme, because his ordinary works convince it. It is true, that a little philosophy inclineth man's minde to Atheisme; but depth in philosophy bringeth men's mindes about to religion. For while the minde of man looketh upon second causes scattered, it may sometimes rest in them, and goe no further: but when it beholdeth the chaine of them, confederate and linked together, it must needs flie to Providence and Deitie. Nay even that schoole which is most accused of Atheisme doth most demonstrate religion; that is, the schoole of Leucippus, and Democritus, and Epicurus. For it is a thousand times more credible, that foure mutable elements, and one immutable fift essence, duly and eternally placed, need no God, then that an army of infinite small portions or seedes unplaced, should have produced this order and beauty without a divine Marshall. The Scripture saith; *The foole hath said in his heart, there is no God:* it is not said; *The foole hath thought in his heart:* so as he rather saith it by rote to himselfe, as that he would have, then that he can throughly beleeve it, or be perswaded of it. For none deny there is a God, but those for whom it maketh that there were no God. It appeareth in nothing more, that Atheisme is rather in the lip then in the heart of man, then by this; that Atheists will ever be talking of that their opinion, as if they fainted in it within themselves, and would be glad to be strengthned by the consent of others. Nay more, you shall have Atheists strive to get disciples, as it fareth with other sects: and, which is most of all, you shall have of them that will suffer for Atheisme, and not recant; whereas if they did truly thinke that there were no such thing as God, why should they trouble themselves? Epicurus is charged that he did but dissemble, for his credit's sake, when he affirmed there were blessed natures, but such as enjoyed themselves without having respect to the government of the world. Wherin they say he did temporize; though in secret he thought there was no God. But certainly, he is traduced; for his words are noble and divine: *Non Deos vulgi negare profanum; sed vulgi opiniones Diis applicare profanum.* Plato could have said no more. And although he had the confidence to deny the administration, he had not the power to deny the nature. The Indians of the West have names for their particular gods, though they have no name for God: as if the heathens should have had the names Jupiter, Apollo, Mars, etc. but not the word Deus: which shewes that even those barbarous people have the notion, though they have not the latitude and extent of it. So that against Atheists the very savages take part with the very subtillest philosophers. The contemplative Atheist is rare; a Diagoras, a Bion, a Lucian perhaps, and some others; and yet they seeme to be more then they are; for that all that impugne a received religion or superstition are by the adverse part branded with the name of Atheists. But the great Atheists indeed are hypocrites; which are ever handling holy things, but without feeling. So as they must needs be cauterized in the end. The causes of Atheisme are; divisions in religion, if they be many; for any one maine division addeth zeale to both sides; but many divisions introduce Atheisme. Another is, scandall of priests; when it is come to that which Saint Bernard saith; *Non est iam dicere, ut Populus, sic Sacerdos: quia nec sic Populus, ut Sacerdos.* A third is, custome of profane scoffing in holy matters; which doth, by little and little, deface the reverence of religion. And lastly, learned times, specially with peace and prosperity: for troubles and adversities doe more bow men's mindes to religion. They that deny a God, destroy man's nobility: For certainly man is of kinne to the beasts by his body; and if he be not of kinne to God, by his spirit, he is a base and ignoble creature. It destroies likewise magnanimity, and the raising of humane nature: for take an example of a dog, and mark what a generosity and courage he will put on when he findes himselfe maintained by a man; who to him is in stead of a God, or *melior natura:* which courage is manifestly such as that creature, without that confidence of a better nature then his owne, could never attaine. So man, when he resteth and assureth himselfe upon divine protection and favour, gathereth a force and faith which humane nature in it selfe could not obtaine. Therefore, as Atheisme is in all respects hatefull, so in this, that it depriveth humane nature of the meanes to exalt it selfe above humane frailty. As it is in particular persons, so it is in nations. Never was there such a State for magnanimity as Rome. Of this State heare what Cicero saith; *Quam volumus licet, patres conscripti, nos amemus, tamen nec numero Hispanos, nec robore Gallos, nec calliditate Pœnos, nec artibus Græcos, nec denique hoc ipso hujus gentis & terræ domestico nativoque sensu Italos ipsos & Latinos; sed pietate, ac religione, atque hac una sapientia, quod deorum immortalium numine omnia regi gubernarique perspeximus, omnes gentes nationesque superavimus.*

❧ Of Superstition.

IT were better to have no opinion of God at all, then such an opinion as is unworthy of him: for the one is Unbeleefe, the other is Contumely: and certainly Superstition is the reproach of the Deity. Plutarch saith well to that purpose: *Surely* (saith he) *I had rather, a great deale, men should say there was no such man at all as Plutarch; then that they should say that there was one Plutarch that would eat his children, as soon as they were borne;* as the poets speake of Saturne. And as the Contumely is greater towards God, so the danger is greater towards men. Atheisme leaves a man to sense; to philosophy; to naturall piety; to lawes; to reputation; all which may be guides to an outward morall vertue, though religion were not; but Superstition dismounts all these and erecteth an absolute monarchy in the mindes of men. Therefore Atheisme did never perturbe States; for it makes men wary of themselves, as looking no further: and we see the times enclined to Atheisme (as the time of Augustus Cæsar) were civil times. But Superstition hath beene the confusion of many States; and bringeth in a new *primum mobile*, that ravisheth all the spheares of government. The master of Superstition is the people; and in all Superstition wise men follow fooles; and arguments are fitted to practise, in a reversed order. It was gravely said, by some of the prelates, in the Councell of Trent, where the doctrine of the Schoolmen bare great sway; *That the schoolemen were like astronomers, which did faigne eccentricks and epicycles, and such engines of orbs, to save the phenomena; though they knew there were no such things:* And, in like manner, that the Schoolmen had framed a number of subtile and intricate axiomes and theorems to save the practise of the Church. The causes of Superstition are: pleasing and sensuall rites and ceremonies: excesse of outward and pharisaicall holinesse; over-great reverence of traditions, which cannot but load the church; the stratagems of prelates for their owne ambition and lucre: the favouring too much of good intentions, which openeth the gate to conceits and novelties; the taking an aime at divine matters by human, which cannot but breed mixture of imaginations; and lastly, barbarous times, especially joyned with calamities and disasters. Superstition, without a vaile, is a deformed thing; for as it addeth deformity to an ape to be so like a man, so the similitude of Superstition to Religion, makes it the more deformed. And as wholesome meat corrupteth to little wormes, so good formes and orders corrupt into a number of petty observances. There is a Superstition in avoiding Superstition, when men thinke to doe best if they goe furthest from the Superstition formerly received: therefore care would be had that (as it fareth in ill purgings) the good be not taken away with the bad; which commonly is done when the people is the reformer.

Of Travaile.

TRAVAILE, in the younger sort, is a part of education; in the elder, a part of experience. He that travaileth into a country, before he hath some entrance into the Language, goeth to Schoole, and not to Travaile. That Young Men Travaile under some Tutor, or grave Servant, I allow well; so that he be such a one that hath the Language, and hath been in the Country before; whereby he may be able to tell them what things are worthy to be seene in the Country where they goe; what acquaintances they are to seeke; what exercises or discipline the place yeeldeth. For else young men shall goe hooded, and looke abroad little. It is a strange thing, that in sea voyages, where there is nothing to be seene but sky and sea, men should make Diaries; but in land-travaile, wherin so much is to be observed, for the most part they omit it; as if chance were fitter to be registred then observation. Let diaries, therefore, be brought in use. The things to be seene and observed are: the courts of Princes, specially when they give audience to ambassadours: the courts of justice, while they sit and heare causes; and so of consistories ecclesiasticke: the churches and monasteries, with the monuments which are therein extant: the wals and fortifications of cities and townes; and so the havens & harbours: antiquities & ruines: libraries; colledges, disputations, and lectures, where any are: shipping & navies: houses, & gardens of state & pleasure, neare great cities: armories: arsenals: magazens: exchanges: burses; ware-houses: exercises of horsemanship; fencing; trayning of souldiers; & the like: comedies, such wherunto the better sort of persons doe resort; treasuries of jewels, and robes; cabinets and rarities: and to conclude, whatsoever is memorable in the places where they goe. After all which the Tutors or Servants ought to make diligent enquirie. As for triumphs; masques; feasts; weddings; funeralls; capitall executions, and such shewes, men need not to be put in mind of them; yet are they not to be neglected. If you will have a young man, to put his Travaile into a little roome, and in short time to gather much, this you must doe. First, as was said, he must have some entrance into the Language before he goeth. Then he must have such a Servant or Tutor as knoweth the Country, as was likewise said. Let him carry with him also some card or booke describing the Country where he travelleth; which will be a good key to his enquiry. Let him keepe also a Diary. Let him not stay long in one citty or towne; more or lesse as the place deserveth, but not long: nay, when he stayeth in one city or towne, let him change his lodging from one end and part of the towne to another; which is a great adamant of acquaintance. Let him sequester himselfe from the company of his country men, and diet in such places where there is good company of the Nation where he Travaileth. Let him upon his removes from one place to another, procure recommendation to some person of quality, residing in the place whither he removeth; that he may use his favour in those things he desireth to see or know. Thus he may abridge his Travaile with much profit. As for the acquaintance which is to be sought in Travaile; that which is most of all profitable is acquaintance with the secretaries and employd men of Ambassadours; for so in Travailing in one country he shall sucke the experience of many. Let him also see and visit eminent persons in all kindes, which are of great name abroad; that he may be able to tell how the life agreeth with the fame. For quarels, they are with care and discretion to be avoided: they are commonly for mistresses; healths; place; and words. And let a man beware how he keepeth company with cholerick and quarelsome persons; for they will engage him into their owne quarels. When a Travailer returneth home, let him not leave the countries where he hath Travailed altogether behinde him; but maintaine a correspondence by letters with those of his acquaintance which are of most worth. And let his Travaile appeare rather in his discourse then in his apparrell or gesture: and in his discourse let him be rather advised in his answers, then forwards to tell stories: and let it appeare that he doth not change his country manners for those of forraigne parts; but onely prick in some flowers of that he hath learned abroad into the customes of his owne Country.

❧ Of Empire.

IT is a miserable state of minde to have few things to desire, and many things to feare: and yet that commonly is the case of Kings; who being at the highest, want matter of desire, which makes their mindes more languishing; and have many representations of perills & shadowes, which makes their mindes the lesse cleare. And this is one reason also of that effect which the Scripture speaketh of; *that the King's heart is inscrutable.* For multitude of jealousies and lack of some predominant desire that should marshall and put in order all the rest, maketh any man's heart hard to finde or sound. Hence it comes likewise that Princes many times make themselves desires, and set their hearts upon toyes: sometimes upon a building; sometimes upon erecting of an order; sometimes upon the advancing of a person; sometimes upon obtaining excellency in some art or feat of the hand; as Nero for playing on the harpe, Domitian for certainty of the hand with the arrow, Commodus for playing at Fence, Caracalla for driving chariots, and the like. This seemeth incredible unto those, that know not the principle; *that the minde of man is more cheared, and refreshed by profiting in small things, then by standing at a stay in great.* We see also that Kings that have been fortunate conquerours in their first yeares, it being not possible for them to goe forward infinitely, but that they must have some checke or arrest in their fortunes, turne in their latter yeares to be superstitious and melancholy: as did Alexander the Great; Dioclesian; and in our memory, Charles the fift; and others: For he that is used to goe forward, and findeth a stop, falleth out of his owne favour, and is not the thing he was.

To speake now of the true temper of Empire: it is a thing rare, & hard to keep: for both temper & distemper consist of contraries. But it is one thing to mingle contraries, another to enterchange them. The answer of Apollonius to Vespasian is full of excellent instruction. Vespasian asked him; *what was Neroe's overthrow?* He answered; *Nero could touch and tune the harpe well; but in government sometimes he used to winde the pins too high, sometimes to let them downe too low.* And certaine it is, that nothing destroieth authority so much as the unequall and untimely enterchange of power pressed too farre, and relaxed too much.

This is true; that the wisdome of all these latter times in Princes' affaires, is rather fine deliveries and shiftings of dangers and mischiefes when they are neare, then solid and grounded courses to keepe them aloofe. But this is but to try masteries with fortune: and let men beware how they neglect and suffer matter of trouble to be prepared: for no man can forbid the sparke, nor tell whence it may come. The difficulties in Princes' businesse, are many and great; but the greatest difficulty is often in their owne minde. For it is common with Princes (saith Tacitus) to will contradictories. *Sunt plerumque regum voluntates vehementes, & inter se contrariæ.* For it is the solœcisme of power, to thinke to command the end, and yet not to endure the meane.

Kings have to deale with their neighbours, their wives, their children, their prelates or clergie, their nobles, their second-nobles or gentlemen, their merchants, their commons, and their men of warre; and from all these arise dangers, if care and circumspection be not used.

First for their neighbours; there can no generall rule be given (the occasions are so variable), save one, which ever holdeth; which is, that Princes doe keepe due centinell, that none of their neighbours doe overgrow so (by encrease of territory, by embracing of trade, by approaches, or the like), as they become more able to annoy them then they were. And this is generally the work of standing counsels to foresee and to hinder it. During that triumvirate of Kings, King Henry the 8. of England, Francis the I. King of France, and Charles the 5. Emperour, there was such a watch kept, that none of the three could win a palme of ground, but the other two would straightwaies ballance it, either by confederation, or, if need were, by a warre; and would not in any wise take up peace at interest. And the like was done by that league (which Guicciardine saith was the security of Italy) made betwene Ferdinando King of Naples, Lorenzius Medices, and Ludovicus Sforza, Potentates, the one of Florence, the other of Millaine. Neither is the opinion of some of the Schoole-Men, to be received; *that a warre cannot justly be made but upon a precedent injury, or provocation.* For there is no question but a just feare of an imminent danger, though there be no blow given, is a lawfull cause of a warre.

For their Wives; there are cruell examples of them. Livia is infamed for the poysoning of her husband; Roxolana, Solyman's wife, was the destruction of that renowned Prince, Sultan Mustapha; and otherwise troubled his house and succession: Edward the Second of England his Queen had the principall hand in the deposing and murther of her husband. This kinde of danger is then to be feared chiefly, when the wives have plots for the raising of their owne children; or else that they be advoutresses.

For their Children: the tragedies likewise of dangers from them have been many. And generally, the entring of fathers into suspicion of their children hath been ever unfortunate. The destruction of Mustapha (that we named before) was so fatall to Solyman's line, as the succession of the Turks from Solyman untill this day is suspected to be untrue, and of strange bloud; for that Selymus the Second was thought to be supposititious. The destruction of Crispus, a young Prince of rare towardnesse, by Constantinus the Great, his father, was in like manner fatall to his house; for both Constantinus and Constance, his sonnes, died violent deaths; and Constantius his other sonne, did little better; who died indeed of sicknesse, but after that Julianus had taken armes against him. The destruction of Demetrius, sonne to Philip the Second of Macedon, turned upon the father, who died of repentance. And many like examples there are: but few or none where the fathers had good by such distrust; except it were, where the sonnes were up in open armes against them; as was Selymus the First against Bajazet; and the three sonnes of Henry the Second, King of England.

For their Prelates; when they are proud and great, there is also danger from them: as it was in the times of Anselmus and Thomas Becket, Archbishops of Canterbury; who with their crosiars did almost try it with the King's sword; and yet they had to deale with stout and haughty Kings; William Rufus, Henry the first, and Henry the second. The danger is not from the State, but where it hath a dependance of forraine authority; or where the churchmen come in and are elected, not by the collation of the King, or particular patrons, but by the people.

For their Nobles; to keepe them at a distance, it is not amisse; but to depresse them, may make a King more absolute, but lesse safe; and lesse able to performe any thing that he desires. I have noted it, in my History of King Henry the Seventh of England, who depressed his Nobility; whereupon it came to passe that his times were full of difficulties and troubles; for the Nobility, though they continued loyall unto him, yet did they not co-operate with him in his businesse. So that in effect he was faine to doe all things himselfe.

For their Second Nobles; there is not much danger from them, being a body dispersed. They may sometimes discourse high, but that doth little hurt: besides, they are a counter-poize to the higher Nobility, that they grow not too potent; and lastly, being the most immediate in authority with the common people, they doe best temper popular commotions.

For their Merchants; they are *vena porta;* and if they flourish not, a kingdome may have good limmes, but will have empty veines, and nourish little. Taxes and imposts upon them doe seldome good to the Kings' revenew; for that that he winnes in the hundred he leeseth in the shire; the particular rates being increased, but the totall bulke of trading rather decreased.

For their Commons; there is little danger from them, except it be where they have great and potent heads, or where you meddle with the point of religion, or their customes, or meanes of life.

For their Men of warre; it is a dangerous State, where they live and remaine in a body, and are used to donatives; whereof we see examples in the janizaries & pretorian bands of Rome: but traynings of men, and arming them in severall places, and under severall commanders, and without donatives, are things of defence, and no danger.

Princes are like to heavenly bodies, which cause good or evill times; and which have much veneration, but no rest. All precepts concerning Kings are in effect comprehended, in those two remembrances: *memento quod es homo;* and *memento quod es Deus*, or *vice Dei:* the one bridleth their power, and the other their will.

❧ Of Counsell.

THE greatest trust betweene man and man is the trust of giving Counsell. For in other confidences men commit the parts of life; their lands, their goods, their children, their credit, some particular affaire; but to such, as they make their Counsellours, they commit the whole: by how much the more they are obliged to all faith and integrity. The wisest Princes need not thinke it any diminution to their greatnesse, or derogation to their sufficiency, to rely upon Counsell. God himselfe is not without; but hath made it one of the great names of his blessed Sonne; *The Counsellour*. Salomon hath pronounced, that *in Counsell is stability*. Things will have their first or second agitation; if they be not tossed upon the arguments of Counsell, they will be tossed upon the waves of fortune; and be full of inconstancy, doing and undoing, like the reeling of a drunken man. Salomon's sonne found the force of Counsell, as his father saw the necessity of it. For the beloved kingdome of God was first rent and broken by ill Counsell; upon which Counsell, there are set for our instruction the two markes whereby bad Counsell is for ever best discerned: that it was young Counsell for the persons; and violent Counsell for the matter.

The ancient times doe set forth in figure both the incorporation and inseparable conjunction of Counsel with Kings; and the wise and politique use of Counsell by Kings: the one, in that they say Jupiter did marry Metis, which signifieth Counsell; whereby they intend that Soveraignty is married to Counsell: the other in that which followeth, which was thus: They say after Jupiter was married to Metis, she conceived by him and was with childe; but Jupiter suffered her not to stay till she brought forth, but eat her up; wherby he became himselfe with child, & was delivered of Pallas Armed, out of his head. Which monstrous fable, containeth a secret of Empire; how Kings are to make use of their Councell of State. That first they ought to referre matters unto them, which is the first begetting or impregnation; but when they are elaborate, moulded, and shaped, in the wombe of their Councell, and grow ripe and ready to be brought forth, that then they suffer not their Councell to goe through with the resolution and direction, as if it depended on them; but take the matter backe into their owne hands, and make it appeare to the world that the decrees, and finall directions (which, because they come forth with prudence and power, are resembled to Pallas Armed) proceeded from themselves: and not onely from their authority, but (the more to adde reputation to themselves) from their head and device.

Let us now speake of the Inconveniences of Counsell, and of the Remedies. The Inconveniences that have been noted in calling and using Counsell are three. First, the revealing of affaires, whereby they become lesse secret. Secondly, the weakning of the authority of Princes, as if they were lesse of themselves. Thirdly, the danger of being unfaithfully counselled, and more for the good of them that counsell then of him that is counselled. For which Inconveniences, the doctrine of Italy, and practise of France, in some Kings' times, hath introduced Cabinet Counsels; a remedy worse then the disease.

As to Secrecy; Princes are not bound to communicate all matters with all Counsellors; but may extract and select. Neither is it necessary that he that consulteth what he should doe, should declare what he will doe. But let Princes beware, that the unsecreting of their affaires comes not from themselves. And as for Cabinet Counsels, it may be their motto, *plenus rimarum sum:* one futile person that maketh it his glory to tell, will doe more hurt then many that know it their duty to conceale. It is true there be some affaires which require extreme secrecy, which will hardly go beyond one or two persons besides the King: neither are those Counsels unprosperous: for besides the secrecy, they commonly goe on constantly in one spirit of direction, without distraction. But then it must be a prudent King, such as is able to grinde with a hand-mill; and those Inward Counsellours had need also be wise men, and especially true and trusty to the Kings' ends: as it was with King Henry the Seventh of England, who in his greatest businesse imparted himself to none, except it were to Morton and Fox.

For weakening of authority; the fable sheweth the Remedy. Nay the majesty of Kings is rather exalted then diminished, when they are in the chaire of Counsell: neither was there ever Prince bereaved of his dependances by his Counsell; except where there hath beene either an overgreatnesse in one Counsellour or an overstrict combination in divers; which are things soone found and holpen.

For the last inconvenience, that men will *Counsell with an eye to themselves;* certainly, *non inveniet fidem super terram* is meant of the nature of times, and not of all particular persons. There be that are in nature faithfull, and sincere, and plaine, and direct; not crafty, and involved: let Princes, above all, draw to themselves such natures. Besides, Counsellours are not commonly so united but that one Counsellour keepeth centinell over another; so that if any do Counsell out of faction or private ends, it commonly comes to the King's eare.

But the best remedy is, if Princes know their Counsellours, as well as their Counsellours know them:

Principis est virtus maxima nosse suos.

And on the other side, Counsellours should not be too speculative into their soveraigne's person. The true composition of a Counsellour is rather to be skilfull in their master's businesse, then in his nature; for then he is like to advise him, and not to feede his humour. It is of singular use to Princes if they take the opinions of their Counsell both seperately and together. For private opinion is more free; but opinion before others is more reverend. In private, men are more bold in their owne humours; and in consort, men are more obnoxious to others' humours; therefore it is good to take both: and of the inferiour sort rather in private, to preserve freedome; of the greater, rather in consort, to preserve respect. It is in vaine for Princes to take Counsel concerning matters, if they take no Counsell likewise concerning persons: for all matters are as dead images; and the life of the execution of affaires resteth in the good choice of persons. Neither is it enough to consult concerning persons, *secundum genera*, as in an idea, or mathematicall description, what the kinde and character of the person should be; for the greatest errours are committed, and the most judgement is shewne, in the choice of individuals. It was truly said, *Optimi consiliarii mortui;* books will speake plaine, when Counsellors blanch. Therefore it is good to be conversant in them; specially the bookes of such, as themselves have been actors upon the stage.

The Counsels at this day in most places are but familiar meetings, where matters are rather talked on then debated. And they run too swift to the order or act of Counsell. It were better that in causes of weight, the matter were propounded one day and not spoken to till the next day; *in nocte consilium*. So was it done, in the Commission of Union, between England and Scotland; which was a grave and orderly assembly. I commend set daies for petitions: for both it gives the suitors more certainty for their attendance; and it frees the meetings for matters of estate, that they may *hoc agere*. In choice of committees for ripening businesse for the Counsell, it is better to choose indifferent persons then to make an indifferency by putting in those that are strong on both sides. I commend also standing commissions; as for trade, for treasure, for warre, for suits, for some provinces: for where there be divers particular Counsels, and but one Counsell of estate (as it is in Spaine), they are in effect no more then standing commissions; save that they have greater authority. Let such as are to informe Counsels out of their particular professions (as lawyers, sea-men, mint-men, and the like) be first heard before committees; and then, as occasion serves, before the Counsell. And let them not come in multitudes, or in a tribunitious manner; for that is to clamour Counsels, not to enforme them. A long table and a square table, or seats about the walls, seeme things of forme, but are things of substance; for at a long table a few at the upper end, in effect, sway all the businesse; but in the other forme there is more use of the Counsellours' opinions that sit lower. A King, when he presides in Counsell, let him beware how he opens his owne inclination too much in that which he propoundeth: for else Counsellors will but take the winde of him, and in stead of giving free Counsell, sing him a song of placebo.

❧ Of Delayes.

FORTUNE is like the market; where many times, if you can stay a little, the price will fall. And againe, it is sometimes like Sybilla's offer; which at first offereth the commodity at full, then consumeth part and part, and still holdeth up the price. For *Occasion* (as it is in the common verse) *turneth a bald noddle, after she hath presented her locks in front, and no hold taken:* or at least turneth the handle of the bottle first to be received, and after the belly, which is hard to claspe. There is surely no greater wisedome then well to time the beginnings and onsets of things. Dangers are no more light, if they once seeme light: and more dangers have deceived men then forced them. Nay, it were better to meet some dangers halfe way, though they come nothing neare, then to keepe too long a watch upon their approaches; for if a man watch too long, it is odds he will fall asleepe. On the other side, to be deceived with too long shadowes (as some have beene when the moone was low and shone on their enemies backe), and so to shoot off before the time; or to teach dangers to come on, by over early buckling towards them, is another extreme. The ripenesse or unripenesse of the occasion (as we said) must ever be well weighed; and generally it is good to commit the beginnings of all great actions to Argos with his hundred eyes, and the ends to Briareus with his hundred hands; first to watch, and then to speed. For the helmet of Pluto, which maketh the politicke man goe invisible, is secrecy in the counsell & celerity in the execution. For when things are once come to the execution, there is no secrecy comparable to celerity; like the motion of a bullet in the ayre, which flyeth so swift as it out-runs the eye.

❧ Of Cunning.

WE take Cunning for a sinister or crooked wisedome. And certainly there is great difference between a Cunning man and a Wise man; not onely in point of honesty, but in point of ability. There be that can packe the cards, and yet cannot play well; so there are some that are good in canvasses and factions, that are otherwise weake men. Againe, it is one thing to understand persons, and another thing to understand matters; for many are perfect in men's humours, that are not greatly capable of the reall part of businesse; which is the constitution of one that hath studied men more than bookes. Such men are fitter for practise then for counsell; and they are good but in their own alley: turne them to new men, and they have lost their ayme; so as the old rule to know a foole from a wise man, *Mitte ambos nudos ad ignotos, & videbis*, doth scarce hold for them. And because these Cunning men are like haberdashers of small wares, it is not amisse to set forth their shop.

It is a point of Cunning, to wait upon him with whom you speake, with your eye; as the Jesuites give it in precept: for there be many wise men that have secret hearts and transparant countenances. Yet this would be done, with a demure abasing of your eye sometimes, as the Jesuites also doe use.

Another is, that when you have any thing to obtaine of present dispatch, you entertaine and amuse the party, with whom you deale, with some other discourse; that he be not too much awake to make objections. I knew a Counsellor and Secretary, that never came to Queene Elizabeth of England with bills to signe, but he would alwaies first put her into some discourse of Estate, that she mought the lesse minde the bills.

The like surprize may be made by moving things when the party is in haste, and cannot stay to consider advisedly of that is moved.

If a man would crosse a businesse that he doubts some other would handsomely and effectually move, let him pretend to wish it well, and move it himselfe in such sort as may foile it.

The breaking off in the midst of that one was about to say, as if he tooke himselfe up, breeds a greater appetite in him with whom you conferre, to know more.

And because it workes better when any thing seemeth to be gotten from you by question, then if you offer it of your selfe, you may lay a bait for a question, by shewing another visage and countenance then you are wont; to the end, to give occasion for the party to aske what the matter is of the change? As Nehemias did; *And I had not before that time been sad before the King.*

In things that are tender and unpleasing, it is good to breake the ice by some whose words are of lesse weight, and to reserve the more weighty voice to come in as by chance, so that he may be asked the question upon the other's speech: As Narcissus did, in relating to Claudius the marriage of Messalina and Silius.

In things that a man would not be seen in, himselfe, it is a point of Cunning to borrow the name of the world; as to say; *The world sayes*, or, *There is a speech abroad*. I knew one that, when he wrote a letter, he would put that which was most materiall in the post-script, as if it had been a by-matter.

I knew another that, when he came to have speech, he would passe over that, that he intended most; and goe forth, and come backe againe, and speake of it as of a thing that he had almost forgot.

Some procure themselves to be surprized at such times as it is like the party that they work upon will suddenly come upon them: and to be found with a letter in their hand, or doing somewhat which they are not accustomed; to the end they may be apposed of those things which of themselves they are desirous to utter.

It is a point of Cunning, to let fall those words in a man's owne name, which he would have another man learne and use, and thereupon take advantage. I knew two that were competitors for the Secretaries' place, in Queene Elizabeth's time, and yet kept good quarter betweene themselves; and would conferre, one with another, upon the businesse; and the one of them said, That to be a Secretary, in the *Declination of a monarchy*, was a ticklish thing, and that he did not affect it: the other, straight caught up those words and discoursed with divers of his friends, that he had no reason to desire to be Secretary, in the *Declination of a Monarchy*. The first man tooke hold of it, and found meanes, it was told the Queene; who hearing of a *Declination of a Monarchy*, tooke it so ill as she would never after heare of the others suit.

There is a Cunning, which we in England call, *the turning of the cat in the pan;* which is, when that which a man sayes to another, he laies it as if another had said it to him. And to say truth, it is not easie, when such a matter passed between two, to make it appeare from which of them it first moved and began.

It is a way that some men have, to glaunce and dart at others by justifying themselves, by negatives; as to say, *This I doe not:* as Tigillinus did towards Burrhus; *Se non diversas spes, sed incolumitatem imperatoris simplicitèr spectare.*

Some have in readinesse so many tales and stories, as there is nothing they would insinuate, but they can wrap it into a tale; which serveth both to keepe themselves more in guard, and to make others carry it with more pleasure.

It is a good point of Cunning for a man to shape the answer he would have in his owne words and propositions; for it makes the other party sticke the lesse.

It is strange how long some men will lie in wait, to speake somewhat they desire to say; and how farre about they will fetch; and how many other matters they will beat over, to come neare it. It is a thing of great patience, but yet of much use.

A sudden, bold, and unexpected question, doth many times surprise a man, and lay him open. Like to him that, having changed his name and walking in Pauls, another suddenly came behind him and called him by his true name, whereat straightwaies he looked backe.

But these small wares and petty points of Cunning are infinite: and it were a good deed to make a list of them: for that nothing doth more hurt in a State, then that Cunning men passe for wise.

But certainly some there are that know the resorts and falls of businesse, that cannot sinke into the maine of it: like a house that hath convenient staires and entries, but never a faire roome. Therefore you shall see them finde out pretty looses in the conclusion, but are no waies able to examine or debate matters. And yet commonly they take advantage of their inability, and would be thought wits of direction. Some build rather upon the abusing of others, and (as we now say) *putting tricks upon them*, then upon soundnesse of their own proceedings. But Salomon saith; *Prudens advertit ad gressus suos: stultus divertit ad dolos.*

❧ Of Wisdome.

AN Ant is a wise creature for it selfe, but it is a shrewd thing in an Orchard or Garden. And certainly, men that are great lovers of themselves waste the publique. Divide with reason betweene Selfe-love, and Society: and be so true to thy Selfe, as thou be not false to others; specially to thy King and country. It is a poore center of a man's actions, Himselfe. It is right earth. For that onely stands fast upon his owne center; whereas all things that have affinity with the Heavens, move upon the center of another, which they benefit. The referring of all to a man's Selfe, is more tolerable in a soveraigne Prince; because Themselves are not onely Themselves; but their good and evill is at the perill of the publique fortune. But it is a desperate evill in a servant to a Prince, or a citizen in a republique. For whatsoever affaires passe such a man's hands, he crooketh them to his owne ends: which must needs be often eccentrick to the ends of his master or State. Therefore let Princes, or States, choose such servants as have not this marke; except they meane their service should be made but the accessary. That which maketh the effect more pernicious is that all proportion is lost. It were disproportion enough for the servants good to be preferred before the masters; but yet it is a greater extreme, when a little good of the servant shall carry things against a great good of the masters. And yet that is the case of bad officers, treasurers, ambassadours, generals, and other false and corrupt servants; which set a bias upon their bowle, of their owne petty ends, and envies, to the overthrow of their masters great and important affaires. And for the most part, the good such servants receive is after the modell of their owne fortune; but the hurt they sell for that good is after the modell of their master's fortune. And certainly it is the nature of extreme Selfe-Lovers, as they will set an house on fire, and it were but to roast their egges: and yet these men many times hold credit with their masters, because their study is but to please them and profit Themselves; and for either respect they will abandon the good of their affaires.

Wisdome for a Man's Selfe is, in many branches thereof, a depraved thing. It is the Wisedome of rats, that will be sure to leave a house somewhat before it fall. It is the Wisedome of the fox, that thrusts out the badger, who digged and made roome for him. It is the Wisedome of crocodiles, that shed teares when they would devoure. But that which is specially to be noted is, that those which (as Cicero saies of Pompey) are *sui amantes sine rivali*, are many times unfortunate. And whereas they have all their time sacrificed to Themselves, they become in the end themselves sacrifices to the inconstancy of fortune; whose wings they thought, by their Self-Wisedome, to have pinioned.

❧ Of Innovations.

AS the births of living creatures at first are ill shapen: so are all Innovations, which are the births of time. Yet notwithstanding, as those that first bring honour into their family are commonly more worthy then most that succeed, so the first president (if it be good) is seldome attained by imitation. For Ill, to man's nature as it stands perverted, hath a naturall motion, strongest in continuance: but Good, as a forced motion, strongest at first. Surely every medicine is an Innovation; and he that will not apply new remedies must expect new evils: for Time is the greatest Innovatour: and if Time, of course, alter things to the worse, and Wisedome and Counsell shall not alter them to the better, what shall be the end? It is true, that what is setled by Custome, though it be not good, yet at least it is fit. And those things which have long gone together, are as it were confederate within themselves: whereas new things peece not so well; but though they helpe by their utility, yet they trouble by their inconformity. Besides, they are like strangers; more admired, and less favoured. All this is true, if time stood still; which contrariwise moveth so round, that a froward retention of Custome is as turbulent a thing, as an Innovation: and they that reverence too much Old Times, are but a scorne to the New. It were good therefore that men in their Innovations would follow the example of Time it selfe; which indeed Innovateth greatly, but quietly, and by degrees scarce to be perceived. For otherwise, whatsoever is new is unlooked for; and ever it mends some and paires other: and he that is holpen takes it for a Fortune, and thanks the

Time; and he that is hurt, for a wrong, and imputeth it to the Author. It is good also, not to try experiments in States, except the necessity be urgent, or the utility evident: and well to beware that it be the reformation that draweth on the change, and not the desire of change, that pretendeth the reformation. And lastly, that the Novelty, though it be not rejected, yet be held for a suspect: and, as the Scripture saith;

That we make a stand upon the Ancient Way, and
then looke about us, and discover
what is the straight, and
right way, & so to
walke in it.

❧ Of Dispatch.

AFFECTED Dispatch is one of the most dangerous things to businesse that can be. It is like that which the physicians call Predigestion, or Hasty Digestion; which is sure to fill the body full of crudities and secret seeds of diseases. Therefore, measure not Dispatch by the times of sitting, but by the advancement of the businesse. And as in races it is not the large stride or high lift that makes the speed: so in businesse, the keeping close to the matter, and not taking of it too much at once, procureth Dispatch. It is the care of some onely to come off speedily for the time; or to contrive some false periods of businesse, because they may seeme men of Dispatch. But it is one thing to abbreviate by contracting, another by cutting off: and businesse so handled at severall sittings or meetings goeth commonly backward and forward in an unsteady manner. I knew a wise man that had it for a by-word, when he saw men hasten to a conclusion; *Stay a little, that we may make an end the sooner.*

On the other side, true Dispatch is a rich thing. For time is the measure of businesse, as money is of wares: and businesse is bought at a deare hand where there is small Dispatch. The Spartans and Spaniards have been noted to be of small Dispatch; *Mi venga la muerte de Spagna; Let my death come from Spaine;* for then it will be sure to be long in comming.

Give good hearing to those that give the first information in businesse; and rather direct them in the beginning then interrupt them in the continuance of their speeches: for he that is put out of his owne order will goe forward and backward, and be more tedious while he waits upon his memory, then he could have been if he had gone on in his owne course. But sometimes it is seene that the moderator is more troublesome then the actor.

Iterations are commonly losse of time. But there is no such gaine of time as to iterate often the state of the question: for it chaseth away many a frivolous speech as it is comming forth. Long and curious speeches are as fit for Dispatch as a robe or mantle with a long traine is for race. Prefaces, and passages, and excusations, and other speeches of reference to the person, are great wasts of time; and though they seeme to proceed of modesty, they are bravery. Yet beware of being too materiall, when there is any impediment or obstruction in men's wils; for pre-occupation of minde ever requireth preface of speech; like a fomentation to make the unguent enter.

Above all things, Order, and Distribution, and Singling out of Parts, is the life of Dispatch; so as the Distribution be not too subtill: for he that doth not divide will never enter well into businesse; and he that divideth too much will never come out of it clearely. To choose time is to save time; and an unseasonable motion is but beating the ayre. There be three parts of businesse: the Preparation; the Debate or Examination; and the Perfection. Whereof, if you looke for Dispatch, let the middle onely be the worke of many, and the first and last the worke of few. The proceeding upon somewhat conceived in writing doth for the most part facilitate Dispatch: for though it should be wholly rejected, yet that negative is more pregnant of direction, then an indefinite; as ashes are more generative then dust.

❧ Of Seeming Wise.

IT hath been an opinion, that the French are wiser then they seeme; and the Spaniards seeme wiser then they are. But howsoever it be between nations, certainly it is so between man and man. For as the Apostle saith of Godlinesse; *Having a shew of godlinesse, but denying the power thereof;* so certainly there are in point of wisedome and sufficiency, that doe nothing or little, very solemnly; *magno conatu nugas.* It is a ridiculous thing and fit for a satyre to persons of judgement, to see what shifts these formalists have, and what prospectives, to make superficies to seeme body, that hath depth and bulke. Some are so close and reserved, as they will not shew their wares but by a darke light; and seeme alwaies to keepe backe somewhat; and when they know within themselves they speake of that they doe not well know, would neverthelesse seeme to others to know of that which they may not well speake. Some helpe themselves with countenance and gesture, and are wise by signes; as Cicero saith of Piso, that when he answered him, he fetched one of his browes up to his forehead, & bent the other downe to his chin. *Respondes, altero ad frontem sublato, altero ad mentum depresso supercilio; crudelitatem tibi non placere.* Some thinke to beare it by speaking a great word, and being peremptory; and goe on, and take by admittance that which they cannot make good. Some, whatsoever is beyond their reach, will seeme to despise or make light of it, as impertinent or curious; and so would have their ignorance seeme judgement. Some are never without a difference, and commonly by amusing men with a subtilty, blanch the matter; of whom A. Gellius saith; *Hominem delirum, qui verborum minutiis rerum frangit pondera.* Of which kinde also, Plato in his Protagoras bringeth in Prodicus, in scorne, and maketh him make a speech that consisteth of distinctions from the beginning to the end. Generally, such men in all deliberations finde ease to be of the negative side, and affect a credit to object and foretell difficulties: for when propositions are denied, there is an end of them; but if they be allowed, it requireth a new worke: which false point of wisedome, is the bane of businesse. To conclude, there is no decaying merchant, or inward beggar, hath so many tricks to uphold the credit of their wealth, as these empty persons have to maintaine the credit of their sufficiency. Seeming Wise-men may make shift to get opinion: but let no man choose them for employment; for certainly you were better take for businesse a man somewhat absurd then over formall.

Of Frendship.

IT had beene hard for him that spake it, to have put more truth and untruth together in few words, then in that speech; *Whosoever is delighted in solitude is either a wilde beast or a God.* For it is most true that a naturall and secret hatred and aversation towards society in any man, hath somewhat of the savage beast; but it is most untrue that it should have any character at all of the Divine Nature; except it proceed not out of a pleasure in Solitude, but out of a love and desire, to sequester a man's selfe for a higher conversation: such as is found to have been falsely and fainedly in some of the heathen; as Epimenides the Candian, Numa the Roman, Empedocles the Sicilian, and Apollonius of Tyana; and truly and really, in divers of the ancient hermits, and Holy Fathers of the Church. But little doe men perceive, what Solitude is and how farre it extendeth. For a crowd is not company; and faces are but a gallery of pictures; and talke but a tinckling cymball, where there is no love. The Latine adage meeteth with it a little; *Magna civitas, magna solitudo;* because in a great Towne, Frends are scattered; so that there is not that fellowship, for the most part, which is in lesse Neighbourhoods. But we may goe further, and affirme most truly, that it is a meere and miserable solitude, to want true Frends; without which the world is but a wildernesse: and even in this sense also of Solitude, whosoever in the frame of his nature and affections is unfit for Frendship, he taketh it of the beast, and not from humanity.

A principall Fruit of Frendship is the ease and discharge of the fulnesse and swellings of the heart, which passions of all kinds doe cause and induce. We know diseases of stoppings and suffocations are the most dangerous in the body; and it is not much otherwise in the minde: you may take sarza to open the liver; steele to open the spleene; flowers of sulphur for the lungs; castoreum for the braine; but no receipt openeth the heart, but a true Frend; to whom you may impart griefes, joyes, feares, hopes, suspicions, counsels, and whatsoever lieth upon the heart to oppresse it, in a kind of civill shrift or confession.

It is a strange thing to observe how high a rate, great Kings and Monarchs do set upon this Fruit of Frendship, wherof we speake: so great, as they purchase it many times at the hazard of their owne safety and greatnesse. For Princes, in regard of the distance of their fortune from that of their subjects & servants, cannot gather this Fruit; except (to make themselves capable thereof) they raise some persons to be as it were companions and almost equals to themselves, which many times sorteth to inconvenience. The moderne languages give unto such persons the name of Favorites, or Privadoes; as if it were matter of grace, or conversation. But the Roman name attaineth the true use and cause thereof; naming them *participes curarum;* for it is that which tieth the knot. And we see plainly that this hath been done, not by weake and passionate Princes onely, but by the wisest and most politique that ever reigned; who have oftentimes joyned to themselves some of their servants; whom both themselves have called Frends, and allowed others likewise to call them in the same manner; using the word which is received between private men.

L. Sylla, when he commanded Rome, raised Pompey (after surnamed the Great) to that height, that Pompey vaunted himselfe for Sylla's overmatch. For when he had carried the consulship for a frend of his, against the pursuit of Sylla, and that Sylla did a little resent thereat, and began to speake great, Pompey turned upon him againe, and in effect bad him be quiet; *for that more men adored the Sunne rising, then the Sunne setting*. With Julius Cæsar, Decimus Brutus had obtained that interest, as he set him downe in his testament for heire in remainder after his nephew. And this was the man that had power with him to draw him forth to his death. For when Cæsar would have discharged the Senate, in regard of some ill presages, & specially a dreame of Calpurnia; this man lifted him gently by the arme out of his chaire, telling him he hoped he would not dismisse the Senate till his wife had dreamt a better dreame. And it seemeth his favour was so great, as Antonius, in a letter which is recited *verbatim* in one of Cicero's Philippiques, calleth him *venefica, witch;* as if he had enchanted Cæsar. Augustus raised Agrippa (though of meane birth) to that heighth, as when he consulted with Mæcenas, about the marriage of his daughter Julia, Mæcenas tooke the liberty to tell him, *that he must either marry his daughter to Agrippa, or take away his life; there was no third way, he had made him so great.* With Tiberius Cæsar, Sejanus had ascended to that height, as they two were tearmed and reckoned as a paire of Frends. Tiberius in a letter to him saith; *Hæc pro Amicitia nostra non occultavi:* and the whole Senate dedicated an altar to Frendship, as to a goddesse, in respect of the great dearenesse of Frendship between them two. The like or more was between Septimius Severus and Plautianus. For he forced his eldest sonne to marry the daughter of Plautianus; and would often maintaine Plautianus in doing affronts to his son: and did write also in a letter to the Senate, by these words; *I love the man so well, as I wish he may over-live me.* Now if these Princes had beene as a

Trajan or a Marcus Aurelius, a man might have thought that this had proceeded of an abundant goodnesse of nature; but being men so wise, of such strength and severitie of minde, and so extreme lovers of themselves, as all these were, it proveth most plainly that they found their owne felicitie (though as great as ever happened to mortall men) but as an halfe peece, except they mought have a Frend to make it entire: and yet, which is more, they were Princes, that had wives, sonnes, nephews; and yet all these could not supply the comfort of Frendship.

It is not to be forgotten, what Commineus observeth of his first master, Duke Charles the Hardy; namely, that hee would communicate his secrets with none; and least of all, those secrets which troubled him most. Whereupon he goeth on and saith that towards his latter time; *that closenesse did impaire & a little perish his understanding*. Surely Commineus mought have made the same judgement also, if it had pleased him, of his second master, Lewis the Eleventh, whose closenesse was indeed his tormentour. The parable of Pythagoras is darke, but true; *Cor ne edito; Eat not the heart.* Certainly, if a man would give it a hard phrase, those that want Frends to open themselves unto are canniballs of their owne hearts. But one thing is most admirable (wherewith I will conclude this first fruit of Frendship), which is, that this communicating of a man's selfe to his Frend works two contrairie effects; for it redoubleth Joyes, and cutteth Griefes in halfes. For there is no man that imparteth his Joyes to his Frend, but he joyeth the more; and no man that imparteth his Griefes to his Frend but hee grieveth the lesse. So that it is, in truth of operation upon a man's minde, of like vertue as the alchymists use to attribute to their stone, for man's bodie; that it worketh all contrary effects, but still to the good and benefit of nature.

But yet, without praying in aid of alchymists, there is a manifest image of this, in the ordinarie course of Nature. For in bodies, union strengthneth & cherisheth any naturall action; and on the other side weakneth and dulleth any violent impression: and even so is it of minds.

The second Fruit of Frendship is healthfull and soveraigne for the Understanding, as the first is for the Affections. For Frendship maketh indeed a faire day in the Affections, from storme and tempests: but it maketh daylight in the Understanding, out of darknesse & confusion of thoughts. Neither is this to be understood onely of faithfull counsell, which a man receiveth from his Frend; but before you come to that, certaine it is that whosoever hath his minde fraught with many thoughts, his wits and understanding doe clarifie and breake up, in the communicating and discoursing with another; he tosseth his thoughts more easily; he marshalleth them more orderly; he seeth how they looke when they are turned into words. Finally, he waxeth wiser then himselfe; and that more by an houre's discourse then by a daye's meditation. It was well said by Themistocles to the King of Persia; *That speech was like cloth of Arras, opened and put abroad; whereby the imagery doth appeare in figure; whereas in thoughts, they lie but as in packs.* Neither is this second Fruit of Frendship, in opening the understanding, restrained onely to such Frends as are able to give a man counsell: (they indeed are best); but even without that, a man learneth of himselfe, and bringeth his owne thoughts to light, and whetteth his wits as against a stone, which it selfe cuts not. In a word, a man were better relate himselfe to a statua or picture, then to suffer his thoughts to passe in smother.

Adde now, to make this second Fruit of Frendship compleat, that other point which lieth more open and falleth within vulgar observation; which is Faithfull Counsell from a Frend. Heraclitus saith well, in one of his Ænigmæs; *Dry light is ever the best.* And certaine it is, that the light that a man receiveth by Counsell from another is drier and purer then that which commeth from his owne understanding and judgement; which is ever infused and drenched in his affections and customes. So as there is as much difference betweene the Counsell that a Frend giveth, and that a man giveth himselfe, as there is between the Counsell of a Frend and of a flatterer. For there is no such flatterer as is a man's selfe; and there is no such remedy against flattery of a man's selfe as the liberty of a Frend. Counsell is of two sorts: the one concerning Manners, the other concerning Businesse. For the first, the best preservative to keepe the minde in health is the faithfull admonition of a Frend. The calling of a man's selfe to a strict account is a medicine, sometime too piercing and corrosive. Reading good bookes of morality is a little flat and dead. Observing our faults in others is sometimes unproper for our case. But the best receipt (best, I say, to worke, and best to take) is the admonition of a Frend. It is a strange thing to behold what grosse errours and extreme absurdities many (especially of the greater sort) doe commit, for want of a Frend to tell them of them; to the great dammage both of their fame and fortune. For, as S. James saith, they are as men *that looke sometimes into a glasse, and presently forget their own shape and favour*. As for businesse, a man may think, if he will, that two eyes see no more then one; or that a gamester seeth alwaies more then a looker on; or that a man in anger is as wise as he that hath said over the foure and twenty letters; or that a musket may be shot off as well upon the arme as upon a rest; and such other fond and high imaginations, to thinke himselfe all in all. But when all is done, the helpe of good Counsell is that which setteth businesse straight. And if any man thinke that he will take Counsell, but it shall be by peeces; asking Counsell in one businesse of one man, and in another businesse of another man; it is well (that is to say, better perhaps then if he asked none at all); but he runneth two dangers: one, that he shall not be faithfully counselled; for it is a rare thing, except it be from a perfect and entire Frend, to have Counsell given, but such as shalbe bowed and crooked to some ends which he hath that giveth it. The other, that he shall have Counsell given, hurtfull and unsafe (though with good meaning), and mixt partly of mischiefe and partly of remedy: even as if you would call a physician that is thought good for the cure of the disease you complaine of, but is unacquainted with your body; and therefore may put you in way for a present cure but overthroweth your health in some other kinde; and so cure the disease and kill the patient. But a Frend that is wholly acquainted with a man's estate will beware, by furthering any present businesse, how he dasheth upon other inconvenience. And therefore rest not upon Scattered Counsels; they will rather distract and misleade, then settle and direct.

After these two noble Fruits of Frendship; (Peace in the Affections and Support of the Judgement) followeth the last Fruit; which is like the pomgranat, full of many kernels; I meane Aid and Bearing a Part in all actions, and occasions. Here the best way to represent to life the manifold use of Frendship is to cast and see how many things there are which a man cannot doe himselfe; and then it will appeare that it was a sparing speech of the Ancients, to say, *that a Frend is another himselfe:* for that a Frend is farre more then himselfe. Men have their time, and die many times in desire of some things which they principally take to heart; the bestowing of a child, the finishing of a worke, or the like. If a man have a true Frend, he may rest almost secure that the care of those things will continue after him. So that a man hath as it were two lives in his desires. A man hath a body, and that body is confined to a place; but where Frendship is, all offices of life are as it were granted to him and his deputy. For he may exercise them by his Frend. How many things are there which a man cannot, with any face or comelines, say or doe himselfe? A man can scarce alledge his owne merits with modesty, much lesse extoll them: a man cannot sometimes brooke to supplicate or beg: and a number of the like. But all these things are gracefull in a Frend's mouth, which are blushing in a man's owne. So againe, a man's person hath many proper relations which he cannot put off. A man cannot speake to his sonne but as a father; to his wife but as a husband; to his enemy but upon termes: whereas a Frend may speak as the case requires, and not as it sorteth with the person. But to enumerate these things were endlesse: I have given the rule, where a man cannot fitly play his owne part: if he have not a Frend, he may quit the stage.

❧ Of Expence.

RICHES are for spending, and spending for honour and good actions. Therefore extraordinary Expence must be limitted by the worth of the occasion: for voluntary undoing may be as well for a man's country as for the Kingdome of Heaven. But ordinary Expence ought to be limitted by a man's estate; and governed with such regard, as it be within his compasse; and not subject to deceit and abuse of servants; and ordered to the best shew, that the bils may be lesse then the estimation abroad. Certainly, if a man will keep but of even hand, his ordinary Expences ought to be but to the halfe of his receipts; and if he thinke to waxe rich, but to the third part. It is no basenesse for the greatest to descend and looke into their owne Estate. Some forbeare it, not upon negligence alone, but doubting to bring themselves into melancholy, in respect they shall finde it broken. But wounds cannot be cured without searching. He that cannot looke into his own Estate at all, had need both choose well those whom he employeth, and change them often: for new are more timorous and lesse subtile. He that can looke into his Estate but seldome, it behoveth him to turne all to certainties. A man had need, if he be plentifull in some kinde of Expence, to be as saving againe in some other. As if he be plentifull in diet, to be saving in apparell: if he be plentifull in the hall, to be saving in the stable; and the like. For he that is plentifull in Expences of all kindes will hardly be preserved from decay. In clearing of a man's Estate, he may as well hurt himselfe in being too sudden, as in letting it runne on too long. For hasty selling is commonly as disadvantageable as interest. Besides, he that cleares at once will relapse; for finding himselfe out of straights he will revert to his customes: but hee that cleareth by degrees induceth a habite of frugalitie, and gaineth as well upon his minde as upon his Estate. Certainly, who hath a State to repaire, may not despise small things: and commonly it is lesse dishonourable to abridge pettie charges then to stoope to pettie gettings. A man ought warily to beginne charges which once begun will continue: but in matters that returne not he may be more magnificent.

❧ Of the true Greatnesse of Kingdomes and Estates.

THE speech of Themistocles the Athenian, which was haughtie and arrogant, in taking so much to himselfe, had been a grave and wise observation and censure, applied at large to others. Desired at a feast to touch a lute, he said; *He could not fiddle, but yet he could make a small towne a great citty.* These words (holpen a little with a metaphore) may expresse two differing abilities in those that deale in businesse of Estate. For if a true survey be taken of Counsellours and Statesmen, there may be found (though rarely) those which can make a small State great, and yet cannot fiddle: as on the other side, there will be found a great many that can fiddle very cunningly, but yet are so farre from being able to make a small State great, as their gift lieth the other way; to bring a great and flourishing Estate to ruine and decay. And certainly those degenerate arts and shifts, whereby many Counsellours and Governours gaine both favour with their masters and estimation with the vulgar, deserve no better name then fiddling; being things rather pleasing for the time, and gracefull to themselves onely, then tending to the weale and advancement of the State which they serve. There are also (no doubt) Counsellours and Governours which may be held sufficient (*negotiis pares*) able to mannage affaires, and to keepe them from precipices and manifest inconveniences; which neverthelesse are farre from the abilitie to raise and amplifie an Estate in power, meanes, and fortune. But be the worke-men what they may be, let us speake of the worke; that is, the true Greatnesse of Kingdomes and Estates; and the meanes thereof. An argument fit for great and mightie Princes to have in their hand; to the end that neither by over-measuring their forces, they leese themselves in vaine enterprises; nor on the other side, by undervaluing them, they descend to fearefull and pusillanimous counsells.

The Greatnesse of an Estate in bulke and territorie, doth fall under measure; and the Greatnesse of finances and revenew doth fall under computation. The population may appeare by musters: and the number and greatnesse of cities and townes by cards and maps. But yet there is not any thing amongst civill affaires more subject to errour then the right valuation and true judgement concerning the power and forces of an Estate. The Kingdome of Heaven is compared, not to any great kernell or nut, but to a graine of mustard seed; which is one of the least graines, but hath in it a propertie and spirit hastily to get up and spread. So are there States great in territorie, and yet not apt to enlarge or command; and some that have but a small dimension of stemme, and yet apt to be the foundations of great monarchies.

Walled townes, stored arcenalls and armouries, goodly races of horse, chariots of warre, elephants, ordnance, artillery, and the like: all this is but a sheep in a lion's skin, except the breed and disposition of the people be stout and warlike. Nay number (it selfe) in armies importeth not much, where the people is of weake courage: for (as Virgil saith) *it never troubles a wolfe, how many the sheepe be.* The armie of the Persians in the plaines of Arbela was such a vast sea of people, as it did somewhat astonish the commanders in Alexander's armie;

who came to him therefore, and wisht him to set upon them by night; but hee answered, *He would not pilfer the victory.* And the defeat was easie. When Tigranes the Armenian, being incamped upon a hill with 400000 men, discovered the armie of the Romans, being not above 14000, marching towards him, he made himselfe merry with it, and said; *Yonder men are too many for an ambassage, and too few for a fight.* But before the sunne sett, he found them enough to give him the chace with infinite slaughter. Many are the examples of the great oddes between number and courage: so that a man may truly make a judgement; that the principal point of Greatnesse in any State is to have a race of military men. Neither is money the sinewes of warre (as it is trivially said), where the sinewes of men's armes, in base and effeminate people, are failing. For Solon said well to Crœsus (when in ostentation he shewed him his gold) *Sir, if any other come that hath better iron then you, he will be master of all this gold.* Therefore let any Prince or State thinke soberly of his forces, except his militia of natives be of good and valiant soldiers. And let Princes, on the other side, that have subjects of martiall disposition, know their owne strength; unlesse they be otherwise wanting unto themselves. As for mercenary forces (which is the helpe in this case), all examples shew that, whatsoever Estate or Prince doth rest upon them; *hee may spread his feathers for a time, but he will mew them soone after.*

The blessing of Judah and Issachar will never meet; *that the same people or nation should be both the lion's whelpe and the asse between burthens:* neither will it be, that a people over-laid with taxes should ever become valiant and martiall. It is true that taxes levied by consent of the Estate, doe abate men's courage lesse; as it hath beene seene notably in the excises of the Low Countries; and in some degree, in the subsidies of

England. For you must note that we speake now of the heart and not of the purse. So that although the same tribute and tax, laid by consent or by imposing, be all one to the purse; yet it workes diversly upon the courage. So that you may conclude; *that no people over-charged with tribute is fit for Empire.*

Let States that aime at Greatnesse take heed how their Nobility and Gentlemen doe multiply too fast. For that maketh the common subject grow to be a peasant and base swaine, driven out of heart, & in effect but the Gentleman's labourer. Even as you may see in coppice woods; *if you leave your staddles too thick, you shall never have cleane underwood, but shrubs and bushes.* So in countries, if the Gentlemen be too many, the Commons will be base; and you will bring it to that, that not the hundred poll will be fit for an helmet; especially as to the infantery, which is the nerve of an army; and so there will be great population and little strength. This which I speake of hath been no where better seen then by comparing of England and France; whereof England, though farre lesse in territory and population, hath been (neverthelesse) an overmatch; in regard the Middle People of England make good souldiers, which the Peasants of France doe not. And herein the device of King Henry the Seventh (whereof I have spoken largely in the *History of his Life*) was profound and admirable; in making farmes and houses of husbandry of a standard; that is, maintained with such a proportion of land unto them, as may breed a subject to live in convenient plenty and no servile condition; and to keepe the plough in the hands of the owners, and not meere hirelings. And thus indeed you shall attaine to Virgil's character, which he gives to ancient Italy.

—Terra potens armis atque ubere glebæ.

Neither is that State (which for any thing I know, is almost peculiar to England, and hardly to be found any where else, except it be perhaps in Poland) to be passed over; I meane the State of Free Servants and Attendants upon Noblemen and Gentlemen; which are no waies inferiour unto the yeomanry for armes. And therefore out of all question, the splendour and magnificence and great retinues and hospitality of Noblemen and Gentlemen, received into custome, doth much conduce unto martiall greatnesse. Whereas, contrariwise, the close and reserved living of Noblemen and Gentlemen causeth a penury of military forces.

By all meanes it is to be procured, that the trunck of Nebuchadnezzar's tree of Monarchy be great enough to beare the branches and the boughes; that is, that the Naturall Subjects of the Crowne or State beare a sufficient proportion to the Stranger Subjects that they governe. Therfore all States that are liberall of naturalization towards strangers are fit for Empire. For to thinke that an handfull of people can, with the greatest courage and policy in the world, embrace too large extent of dominion, it may hold for a time, but it will faile suddainly. The Spartans were a nice people in point of naturalization; whereby, while they kept their compasse, they stood firme; but when they did spread, and their boughs were becommen too great for their stem, they became a windfall upon the suddaine. Never any State was in this point so open to receive strangers into their body as were the Romans. Therefore it sorted with them accordingly; for they grew to the greatest Monarchy. Their manner was, to grant naturalization (which they called *jus civitatis*) and to grant it in the highest degree; that is, not onely *jus commercii*, *jus connubii*, *jus hæreditatis;* but also, *jus suffragii*, and *jus honorum.* And this not to singular persons alone, but likewise to whole families; yea to cities, and sometimes to nations. Adde to this their custome of plantation of colonies; whereby the Roman plant was removed into the soile of other nations. And putting both constitutions together, you will say that it was not the Romans that spred upon the World; but it was the World that spred upon the Romans: and that was the sure way of Greatnesse. I have marveiled sometimes at Spaine, how they claspe and containe so large dominions, with so few naturall Spaniards: but sure the whole compasse of Spaine is a very great body of a tree; farre above Rome and Sparta at the first. And besides, though they have not had that usage to naturalize liberally, yet they have that which is next to it; that is, to employ almost indifferently all nations in their militia of ordinary soldiers; yea, and sometimes in their highest commands. Nay it seemeth at this instant they are sensible of this want of natives; as by the Pragmaticall Sanction, now published, appeareth.

It is certaine that sedentary and within-doore arts, and delicate manufactures (that require rather the finger then the arme), have in their nature a contrariety to a military disposition. And generally, all warlike people are a little idle and love danger better than travaile. Neither must they be too much broken of it, if they shall be preserved in vigour. Therefore, it was great advantage in the ancient States of Sparta, Athens, Rome, and others, that they had the use of Slaves; which commonly did rid those manufactures. But that is abolished, in greatest part, by the Christian law. That which commeth nearest to it is to leave those arts chiefly to strangers, (which for that purpose are the more easily to be received) and to containe the principall bulke of the vulgar natives within those three kinds; tillers of the ground; free servants; & handy-crafts-men of strong & manly arts, as smiths, masons, carpenters, &c; not reckoning professed souldiers.

But above all, for Empire and Greatnesse, it importeth most, that a nation doe professe armes as their principall honour, study, and occupation. For the things which we formerly have spoken of are but habilitations towards armes; and what is habilitation without intention and act? Romulus, after his death (as they report or faigne) sent a present to the Romans, that above all they should intend armes; and then they should prove the greatest Empire of the world. The fabrick of the State of Sparta was wholly (though not wisely) framed and composed to that scope and end. The Persians and Macedonians had it for a flash. The Galls, Germans, Goths, Saxons, Normans, and others, had it for a time. The Turks have it at this day, though in great declination. Of Christian Europe, they that have it are, in effect, onely the Spaniards. But it is so plaine, *that every man profiteth in that hee most intendeth*, that it needeth not to be stood upon. It is enough to point at it; that no nation which doth not directly professe armes may looke to have Greatnesse fall into their mouths. And on the other side, it is a most certaine oracle of time; that those States, that continue long in that profession (as the Romans and Turks principally have done) do wonders. And those that have professed armes but for an age, have notwithstanding commonly attained that Greatnesse in that age which maintained them long after when their profession and exercise of armes hath growen to decay.

Incident to this point is, for a State to have those lawes or customes which may reach forth unto them, just occasions (as may be pretended) of warre. For there is that justice imprinted in the nature of men, that they enter not upon wars (whereof so many calamities doe ensue) but upon some, at the least specious, grounds and quarells. The Turke hath at hand, for cause of warre, the propagation of his law or sect; a quarrel that he may alwaies command. The Romans, though they esteemed the extending the limits of their empire to be great honour to their generalls when it was done, yet they never rested upon that alone to begin a warre. First therefore, let nations that pretend to Greatnesse have this; that they be sensible of wrongs, either upon borderers, merchants, or politique ministers; and that they sit not too long upon a provocation. Secondly, let them be prest and ready to give aids and succours to their confederates: as it ever was with the Romans: in so much, as if the confederate had leagues defensive with divers other States, and upon invasion offered did implore their aides severally, yet the Romans would ever bee the formost, and leave it to none other to have the honour. As for the warres which were anciently made on the behalfe of a kinde of partie, or tacite conformitie of Estate, I doe not see how they may be well justified: as when the Romans made a warre for the libertie of Grecia: or when the Lacedemonians and Athenians made warres to set up or pull downe Democracies and Oligarchies: or when warres were made by forrainers, under the pretence of justice or protection, to deliver the subjects of others from tyrannie and oppression; and the like. Let it suffice, that no Estate expect to be Great that is not awake upon any just occasion of arming.

No body can be healthfull without exercise, neither naturall body nor politique: and certainly to a Kingdome or Estate, a just and honourable warre is the true exercise. A civill warre, indeed, is like the heat of a feaver; but a forraine warre is like the heat of exercise, and serveth to keepe the body in health: for in a slothfull peace, both courages will effeminate and manners corrupt. But howsoever it be for happinesse, without all question, for Greatnesse it maketh, to bee still for the most part in armes: and the strength of a veteran armie (though it be a chargeable businesse) alwaies on foot is that which commonly giveth the law, or at least the reputation, amongst all neighbour States; as may well bee seene in Spaine; which hath had, in one part or other, a veteran armie almost continually, now by the space of six-score yeeres.

To be master of the Sea is an abridgement of a Monarchy. Cicero writing to Atticus, of Pompey his preparation against Cæsar, saith; *Consilium Pompeii plane Themistocleum est; putat enim, qui Mari potitur, cum rerum potiri.* And, without doubt, Pompey had tired out Cæsar, if upon vaine confidence he had not left that way. We see the great effects of battailes by Sea. The battaile of Actium decided the empire of the world. The battaile of Lepanto arrested the Greatnesse of the Turke. There be many examples, where Sea-Fights have beene finall to the warre; but this is when Princes or States have set up their rest upon the battailes. But thus much is certaine; that hee that commands the Sea is at great liberty, and may take as much and as little of the warre as he will. Whereas those that be strongest by land are many times neverthelesse in great straights. Surely, at this day, with us of Europe, the vantage of strength at Sea (which is one of the principall dowries of this Kingdome of Great Brittaine) is great: both because most of the Kingdomes of Europe are not meerely inland, but girt with the Sea most part of their compasse; and because the wealth of both Indies seemes in great part but an accessary to the command of the Seas.

The warres of Latter Ages seeme to be made in the darke, in respect of the glory and honour which reflected upon men from the warres in Ancient Time. There be now, for martiall encouragement, some degrees and orders of chivalry; which neverthelesse are conferred promiscuously upon soldiers & no soldiers; & some remembrance perhaps upon the Scutchion; and some hospitals for maimed soldiers; and such like things. But in Ancient Times, the Trophies erected upon the place of the victory; the funerall Laudatives and Monuments for those that died in the wars; the Crowns and Garlands Personal; the stile of Emperor, which the Great Kings of the world after borrowed; the Triumphes of the Generalls upon their returne; the great Donatives and Largesses upon the disbanding of the armies; were things able to enflame all men's courages. But above all, that of the Triumph, amongst the Romans, was not pageants or gauderie, but one of the wisest and noblest institutions that ever was. For it contained three things; Honour to the Generall; Riches to the Treasury out of the spoiles; and Donatives to the Army. But that honour perhaps were not fit for Monarchies, except it be in the person of the Monarch himselfe, or his sonnes; as it came to passe in the times of the Roman Emperours, who did impropriate the actuall triumphs to themselves and their sonnes, for such wars as they did atchieve in person: and left onely for wars atchieved by subjects, some triumphall garments and ensignes to the Generall.

To conclude; no man can, by *care taking* (as the Scripture saith) *adde a cubite to his stature*, in this little modell of a man's body: but in the great frame of Kingdomes and Common Wealths it is in the power of Princes or Estates to adde amplitude and Greatnesse to their Kingdomes. For by introducing such ordinances, constitutions, and customes, as we have now touched, they may sow Greatnesse to their posteritie and succession. But these things are commonly not observed, but left to take their chance.

❧ Of Regiment of Health.

THERE is a wisdome in this beyond the rules of physicke: a man's owne observation, what he findes good of, and what he findes hurt of, is the best physicke to preserve Health. But it is a safer conclusion to say, *this agreeth not well with me, therefore I will not continue it;* then this, *I finde no offence of this, therefore I may use it.* For strength of nature in youth passeth over many excesses, which are owing a man till his age. Discerne of the comming on of yeares, and thinke not to doe the same things still; for age will not be defied. Beware of sudden change in any great point of diet, and if necessity inforce it, fit the rest to it. For it is a secret both in Nature and State, that it is safer to change many things then one. Examine thy customes of diet, sleepe, exercise, apparell, and the like; and trie, in any thing thou shalt judge hurtfull, to discontinue it by little and little; but so, as if thou doest finde any inconvenience by the change, thou come backe to it againe: for it is hard to distinguish that which is generally held good and wholesome, from that which is good particularly, and fit for thine owne body. To be free minded, and cheerefully disposed, at houres of meat and of sleep and of exercise, is one of the best precepts of long lasting. As for the passions and studies of the minde; avoid envie; anxious feares; anger fretting inwards; subtill and knottie inquisitions; joyes, and exhilarations in excesse; sadnesse not communicated. Entertaine hopes; mirth rather then joy; varietie of delights, rather then surfet of them;

wonder and admiration, and therefore novelties; studies that fill the minde with splendide and illustrious objects, as histories, fables, and contemplations of Nature. If you flie physicke in Health altogether, it will be too strange for your body when you shall need it. If you make it too familiar, it will worke no extraordinary effect when Sicknesse commeth. I commend rather some diet for certaine seasons, then frequent use of physicke, except it be growen into a custome. For those diets alter the body more and trouble it lesse. Despise no new accident, in your body, but aske opinion of it. In Sicknesse, respect Health principally; and in Health, Action. For those that put their bodies to endure in Health, may in most Sicknesses, which are not very sharpe, be cured onely with diet and tendering. Celsus could never have spoken it as a physician, had he not been a wise man withall, when he giveth it for one of the great precepts of health and lasting, that a man doe vary and enterchange contraries, but with an inclination to the more benigne extreme: use fasting and full eating, but rather full eating; watching and sleep, but rather sleep; sitting and exercise, but rather exercise; and the like. So shall Nature be cherished, and yet taught masteries. Physicians are some of them so pleasing and conformable to the humor of the Patient, as they presse not the true cure of the disease; and some other are so regular in proceeding according to art for the disease, as they respect not sufficiently the condition of the Patient. Take one of a middle temper, or if it may not be found in one man, combine two of either sort: and forget not to call as well the best acquainted with your body, as the best reputed of for his faculty.

❧ Of Suspicion.

SUSPICIONS amongst thoughts are like bats amongst birds, they ever fly by twilight. Certainly they are to be repressed, or at the least well guarded: for they cloud the minde; they leese frends; and they checke with businesse, whereby businesse cannot goe on currantly and constantly. They dispose Kings to tyranny, husbands to jealousie, wise men to irresolution and melancholy. They are defects, not in the heart, but in the braine; for they take place in the stoutest natures: as in the example of Henry the Seventh of England: there was not a more Suspicious man, nor a more stout. And in such a composition they doe small hurt. For commonly they are not admitted, but with examination, whether they be likely or no. But in fearefull natures they gaine ground too fast. There is nothing makes a man Suspect much, more then to know little: and therefore men should remedy Suspicion by procuring to know more, and not to keep their Suspicions in smother. What would men have? Doe they thinke those they employ and deale with are saints? Doe they not thinke they will have their owne ends, and be truer to themselves then to them? Therefore, there is no better way to moderate Suspicions, then to account upon such Suspicions as true and yet to bridle them as false. For so farre a man ought to make use of Suspicions, as to provide, as if that should be true that he Suspects, yet it may doe him no hurt. Suspicions that the minde of it selfe gathers are but buzzes; but Suspicions that are artificially nourished, and put into men's heads by the tales and whisprings of others, have stings. Certainly, the best meane to cleare the way in this same wood of Suspicions is francklу to communicate them with the partie that he Suspects: for thereby he shall be sure to know more of the truth of them then he did before; and withall shall make that party more circumspect not to give further cause of Suspicion. But this would not be done to men of base natures: for they, if they finde themselves once suspected, will never be true. The Italian saies, *Sospetto licentia fede:* as if Suspicion did give a pasport to faith: but it ought rather to kindle it to discharge it selfe.

❧ Of Discourse.

SOME in their Discourse desire rather commendation of wit, in being able to hold all arguments, then of judgment, in discerning what is true: as if it were a praise to know what might be said, and not what should be thought. Some have certaine Common Places and Theames wherein they are good, and want variety: which kinde of poverty is for the most part tedious, and when it is once perceived, ridiculous. The honourablest part of talke, is to give the occasion; and againe to moderate and passe to somewhat else; for then a man leads the daunce. It is good, in Discourse and speech of conversation, to vary and entermingle speech of the present occasion with arguments, tales with reasons, asking of questions with telling of opinions; and jest with earnest: for it is a dull thing to tire, and, as we say now, to jade, any thing too farre. As for jest, there be certaine things which ought to be priviledged from it; namely Religion, Matters of State, Great Persons, any man's present Businesse of Importance, and any Case that deserveth Pitty. Yet there be some that thinke their wits have been asleepe, except they dart out somewhat that is piquant, and to the quicke: that is a vaine which would be brideled;

Parce puer stimulis, & fortius utere loris.

And generally, men ought to finde the difference between saltnesse and bitternesse. Certainly, he that hath a Satyricall vaine, as he maketh others afraid of his wit, so he had need be afraid of others' memory. He that questioneth much shall learne much and content much; but especially if he apply his questions to the skill of the persons whom he asketh: for he shall give them occasion to please themselves in speaking, and himselfe shall continually gather knowledge. But let his questions not be troublesome; for that is fit for a poser. And let him be sure to leave other men their turnes to speak. Nay, if there be any that would raigne and take up all the time, let him finde meanes to take them off, and to bring others on; as Musicians use to doe with those that dance too long Galliards. If you dissemble sometimes your knowledge of that you are thought to know, you shall be thought another time to know that you know not. Speach of a man's selfe ought to be seldome, and well chosen. I knew one was wont to say in scorne; *He must needs be a wise man, he speakes so much of himselfe:* and there is but one case wherein a man may commend himselfe with good Grace; and that is in commending Vertue in another; especially, if it be such a Vertue whereunto himselfe pretendeth. Speech of touch towards others should be sparingly used: for Discourse ought to be as a field, without comming home to any man. I knew two Noblemen, of the west part of England, whereof the one was given to scoffe, but kept ever royal cheere in his house: the other would aske of those that had beene at the other's table; *Tell truely, was there never a flout or drie blow given;* To which the guest would answer; *Such and such a thing passed.* The lord would say, *I thought he would marre a good dinner.*

Discretion of Speech is more then Eloquence; & to speak agreeably to him with whom we deale, is more then to speak in good words or in good order. A good continued Speech, without a good Speech of Interlocution, shews slownesse: and a good Reply, or Second Speech, without a good Setled Speech, sheweth shallownesse and weaknesse. As we see in beasts, that those that are weakest in the course are yet nimblest in the turne: as it is betwixt the grey-hound, and the hare. To use too many circumstances ere one come to the matter, is wearisome; to use none at all, is blunt.

❧ Of Plantations.

PLANTATIONS are amongst ancient, primitive, and heroicall Workes. When the world was young it begate more children; but now it is old it begets fewer: for I may justly account new Plantations to be the children of former Kingdomes. I like a Plantation in a pure soile; that is, where people are not Displanted, to the end to Plant in others. For else it is rather an extirpation then a Plantation. Planting of countries is like Planting of woods; for you must make account to leese almost twenty yeeres profit, and expect your recompence in the end. For the principall thing that hath beene the destruction of most Plantations, hath beene the base and hastie drawing of profit in the first yeeres. It is true, speedie profit is not to be neglected, as farre as may stand with the good of the Plantation, but no further. It is a shamefull and unblessed thing to take the scumme of people and wicked condemned men, to be the people with whom you Plant: and not only so, but it spoileth the Plantation; for they will ever live like rogues, and not fall to worke, but be lazie, and doe mischiefe, and spend victuals, and be quickly weary, and then certifie over to their country to the discredit of the Plantation. The people wherewith you Plant ought to be gardners, plough-men, labourers, smiths, carpenters, joyners, fisher-men, fowlers, with some few apothecaries, surgeons, cookes, and bakers. In a country of Plantation, first looke about, what kinde of victuall the countrie yeelds of it selfe to hand: as chestnuts, wallnuts, pine-apples, olives, dates, plummes, cherries, wilde-hony, and the like; and make use of them. Then consider what victuall or esculent things there are, which grow speedily, and within the yeere; as parsnips, carrets, turnips, onions, radish, artichokes of Hierusalem, maiz, and the like. For wheat, barly, and oats, they aske too much Labour: but with pease and beanes you may begin; both because they aske lesse Labour, and because they serve for Meat, as well as for Bread. And of rice likewise commeth a great encrease, and it is a kinde of Meat. Above all, there ought to be brought store of bisket, oat-meale, flower, meale, and the like, in the beginning, till Bread may be had. For beasts or birds, take chiefly such as are least subject to diseases, and multiply fastest: as swine, goats, cockes, hennes, turkies, geese, house-doves, and the like. The victuall in Plantations ought to be expended almost as in a besieged towne; that is, with certaine allowance. And let the maine part of the ground employed to Gardens or Corne, be to a common stocke; and to be laid in, and stored up, & then delivered out in proportion; besides some spots of ground, that any particular person will manure for his owne private. Consider likewise what commodities the soile where the Plantation is doth naturally yeeld, that they may some way helpe to defray the charge of the Plantation: so it be not, as was said, to the untimely prejudice of the maine businesse; as it hath fared with Tobacco in Virginia. Wood commonly aboundeth but too much; and therefore Timber is fit to be one. If there be Iron Ure, and streames whereupon to set the milles, Iron is a brave commoditie where Wood aboundeth. Making of bay salt, if the climate be proper for it, would be put in experience. Growing Silke likewise, if any be, is a likely commoditie. Pitch and tarre, where store of firres and pines are, will not faile. So Drugs and Sweet Woods, where they are, cannot but yeeld great profit. Soape ashes likewise, and other things, that may be thought of. But moile not too much under ground: for the hope of Mines is very uncertaine and useth to make the Planters lazie in other things. For Government, let it be in the hands of one, assisted with some Counsell: and let them have commission to exercise martiall lawes, with some limitation. And above all, let men make the profit of being in the wildernesse, as they have God alwaies, and His service, before their eyes. Let not the Government of the Plantation depend upon too many Counsellours and undertakers, in the countrie that Planteth, but upon a temperate number: and let those be rather Noblemen and Gentlemen, then merchants: for they looke ever to the present gaine. Let there be freedomes from Custome, till the Plantation be of strength: and not only freedome from Custome, but freedome to carrie their commodities where they may make their best of them, except there be some speciall cause of caution. Cramme not in people, by sending too fast company after company; but rather hearken how they waste, and send supplies proportionably; but so, as the number may live well, in the Plantation, and not by surcharge be in penury. It hath beene a great endangering to the health of some Plantations, that they have built along the sea, and rivers, in marish and unwholesome grounds. Therefore, though you begin there, to avoid carriage and other like discommodities, yet build still rather upwards from the streames, then along. It concerneth likewise the health of the Plantation, that they have good store of Salt with them, that they may use it in their victualls, when it shall be necessary. If you Plant where savages are, doe not onely entertaine them with trifles, and gingles; but use them justly and gratiously, with sufficient guard neverthelesse: and doe not winne their favour by helping them to invade their enemies, but for their defence it is not amisse. And send oft of them over to the country that

Plants, that they may see a better condition then their owne, and commend it when they returne. When the Plantation grows to strength, then it is time to Plant with women, as well as with men; that the Plantation may spread into generations, and not be ever peeced from without. It is the sinfullest thing in the world to forsake or destitute a Plantation, once in forwardnesse: for besides the dishonour, it is the guiltinesse of bloud of many commiserable persons.

❧ Of Riches.

I CANNOT call riches better then the Baggage of Vertue. The Roman word is better, *Impedimenta.* For as the Baggage is to an Army, so is Riches to Vertue. It cannot be spared nor left behinde, but it hindreth the march; yea, and the care of it sometimes loseth or disturbeth the victory: of great Riches there is no reall use, except it be in the distribution; the rest is but conceit. So saith Salomon; *Where much is, there are many to consume it; and what hath the owner, but the sight of it with his eyes?* The personall fruition in any man cannot reach to feele great Riches: there is a custody of them; or a power of dole and donative of them; or a fame of them; but no solid use to the owner. Doe you not see what fained prices are set upon little stones and rarities? And what works of ostentation are undertaken, because there might seeme to be some use of great Riches? But then you will say, they may be of use to buy men out of dangers or troubles. As Salomon saith; *Riches are as a strong hold, in the imagination of the rich man.* But this is excellently expressed, that it is Imagination, and not alwaies in Fact. For certainly great Riches have sold more men then they have bought out. Seeke not proud Riches, but such as thou maist get justly, use soberly, distribute cheerefully, and leave contentedly. Yet have no abstract nor friarly contempt of them. But distinguish, as Cicero saith well of Rabirius Posthumus; *In studio rei amplificandæ, apparebat, non avaritiæ prædam, sed instrumentum bonitati, quæri.* Hearken also to Salomon, and beware of hasty gathering of Riches: *Qui festinat ad divitias, non erit insons.* The poets faigne that when

Plutus (which is Riches) is sent from Jupiter, he limps and goes slowly; but when he is sent from Pluto, he runnes and is swift of foot. Meaning that Riches gotten by good meanes and just labour pace slowly; but when they come by the death of others (as by the course of inheritance, testaments, and the like), they come tumbling upon a man. But it mought be applied likewise to Pluto, taking him for the Devill. For when Riches come from the Devill (as by fraud and oppression and unjust meanes), they come upon speed. The waies to enrich are many, and most of them foule. Parsimony is one of the best, and yet is not innocent: for it with-holdeth men from workes of liberality and charity. The improvement of the ground is the most naturall obtaining of Riches; for it is our Great Mother's blessing, the Earth's; but it is slow. And yet where men of great wealth doe stoope to husbandry, it multiplieth Riches exceedingly. I knew a Nobleman in England, that had the greatest audits of any man in my time: a great grasier, a great sheepe-master, a great timber man, a great colliar, a great corne-master, a great lead-man, and so of iron, and a number of the like points of husbandry. So as the earth seemed a sea to him, in respect of the perpetuall importation. It was truly observed by one, that himselfe came very hardly to a little Riches, and very easily to great Riches. For when a man's stocke is come to that, that he can expect the prime of markets, and overcome those bargaines which for their greatnesse are few men's money, and be partner in the industries of younger men, he cannot but encrease mainely. The Gaines of ordinary Trades and Vocations are honest; and furthered by two things chiefly: by diligence; and by a good name for good and faire dealing. But the Gaines of Bargaines are of a more doubtfull nature; when men shall waite upon others' necessity, broake by servants and instruments to draw them on, put off others cunningly that would be better chapmen, and the like practises, which are crafty and naught. As for the Chopping of Bargaines, when a man buies not to hold but to sell over againe, that commonly grindeth double, both upon the seller and upon the buyer. Sharings doe greatly enrich if the hands be well chosen that are trusted. Usury is the certainest meanes of gaine, though one of the worst; as that whereby a man doth eate his bread *in sudore vultus alieni:* and besides, doth plough upon Sundaies. But yet certaine though it be, it hath flawes; for that the scriveners and broakers doe valew unsound men to serve their owne turne. The fortune in being the first in an Invention or in a Priviledge, doth cause sometimes a wonderfull overgrowth in Riches; as it was with the first sugar man in the Canaries. Therefore if a man can play the true logician, to have as well judgement as invention, he may do great matters; especially if the times be fit. He that resteth upon Gaines Certaine shall hardly grow to great Riches: and he that puts all upon Adventures doth often times breake and come to poverty: it is good therefore, to guard Adventures with Certainties, that may uphold losses. Monopolies and Coemption of Wares for Resale, where they are not restrained, are great meanes to enrich; especially if the partie have intelligence what things are like to come into request, and so store himselfe before hand. Riches gotten by Service, though it be of the best rise, yet when they are gotten by flattery, feeding humours, and other servile conditions, they may be placed amongst the worst. As for fishing for Testaments and Executorships (as Tacitus saith of Seneca; *Testamenta et orbos tanquam indagine capi;*) it is yet worse; by how much men submit themselves to meaner persons then in Service. Beleeve not much them that seeme to despise Riches: for they despise them that despaire of them; and none worse, when they come to them. Be not penny-wise; Riches have wings, and sometimes they fly away of themselves, sometimes they must be set flying to bring in more. Men leave their Riches either to their kindred, or to the publique; and moderate portions prosper best in both. A great state left to an heire, is as a lure to all the birds of prey round about to seize on him, if he be not the better stablished in yeares and judgement. Likewise glorious gifts and foundations are like sacrifices without salt; and but the painted sepulchres of Almes, which soone will putrifie and corrupt inwardly. Therefore measure not thine advancements by quantity, but frame them by measure; and deferre not charities till death: for certainly, if a man weigh it rightly, he that doth so, is rather liberall of an other man's, then of his owne.

❧ Of Prophecies.

I MEANE not to speake of Divine Prophecies; nor of heathen oracles; nor of naturall predictions; but only of Prophecies, that have beene of certaine memory, and from hidden causes. Saith the Pythonissa to Saul; *To morrow thou and thy sonne shall be with me.* Homer hath these verses:

At Domus Æneæ cunctis dominabitur oris,
Et nati natorum, & qui nascentur ab illis:

A prophecie, as it seemes, of the Roman Empire. Seneca the Tragedian hath these verses:

——— *Venient annis*
Secula seris, quibus Oceanus
Vincula rerum laxet, & ingens
Pateat Tellus, Typhisque novos
Detegat orbes; nec sit terris
Ultima Thule:

A prophecie of the discovery of America. The daughter of Polycrates dreamed that Jupiter bathed her father, and Apollo annointed him: and it came to passe that he was crucified in an open place, where the sunne made his bodie runne with sweat, and the raine washed it. Philip of Macedon dreamed he sealed up his wive's belly: whereby he did expound it, that his wife should be barren: but Aristander the soothsayer told him his wife was with childe, because men doe not use to seale vessels that are emptie. A phantasme, that appeared to M. Brutus in his tent, said to him; *Philippis iterum me videbis.* Tiberius said to Galba, *Tu quoque, Galba, degustabis imperium.* In Vespasian's time, there went a prophecie in the East; that those that should come forth of Judea, should reigne over the world: which though it may be was meant of our Saviour, yet Tacitus expounds it of Vespasian. Domitian dreamed, the night before he was slaine, that a golden head was growing out of the nape of his necke: and indeed, the succession that followed him for many yeares, made golden times. Henry the Sixt of England said of Henry the Seventh, when he was a lad, and gave him water; *This is the lad that shall enjoy the crowne for which we strive.* When I was in France, I heard from one Dr. Pena, that the Q. Mother, who was given to curious arts, caused the King her husband's nativitie, to be calculated, under a false name; and the astrologer gave a judgement, that he should be killed in a duell; at which the Queene laughed, thinking her husband to be above challenges and duels: but he was slaine, upon a course at tilt, the splinters of the staffe of Mongomery, going in at his bever. The triviall Prophecie, which I heard, when I was a childe and Queene Elizabeth was in the flower of her yeares, was;

When hempe is sponne;
England's done.

Whereby it was generally conceived, that after the Princes had reigned, which had the principiall letters of that word Hempe (which were Henry, Edward, Mary, Philip and Elizabeth) England should come to utter confusion: which, thankes be to God, is verified only in the change of the name: for that the King's stile, is now no more of England, but of Britaine. There was also another Prophecie, before the year of 88. which I doe not well understand.

There shall be seene upon a day.
Betweene the baugh, and the May,
The blacke fleet of Norway.
When that that is come and gone,
England build houses of lime and stone
For after warres shall you have none.

It was generally conceived to be meant of the Spanish fleet that came in '88. For that the King of Spaine's surname, as they say, is Norway. The prediction of Regiomontanus;

Octogessimus octavus mirabilis Annus;

was thought likewise accomplished, in the sending of that great fleet, being the greatest in strength, though not in number, of all that ever swamme upon the Sea. As for Cleon's dreame, I thinke it was a jest. It was, that he was devoured of a long dragon; and it was expounded of a maker of sausages, that troubled him exceedingly. There are numbers of the like kinde; especially if you include Dreames, and Predictions of Astrologie. But I have set downe these few onely of certaine credit, for example. My judgement is, that they ought all to be despised; and ought to serve but for Winter talke by the fire side. Though when I say *despised*, I meane it as for beleefe: for otherwise, the spreading or publishing of them is in no sort to be despised. For they have done much mischiefe: and I see many severe lawes made to suppresse them. That, that hath given them grace, and some credit, consisteth in three things. First, that men marke when they hit, and never marke when they misse: as they doe generally also of Dreames. The second is, that probable conjectures, or obscure traditions, many times turne themselves into Prophecies: while the nature of man, which coveteth Divination, thinkes it no perill to foretell that which indeed they doe but collect. As that of Seneca's verse. For so much was then subject to demonstration, that the globe of the earth had great parts beyond the Atlanticke; which mought be probably conceived not to be all Sea: and adding thereto the tradition in Plato's *Timeus*, and his *Atlanticus*, it mought encourage one, to turne it to a Prediction.

The third, and last (which is the great one) is, that almost all of them, being infinite in number, have beene impostures, and by idle and craftie braines meerely contrived and faigned after the event past.

❧ Of Ambition.

AMBITION is like Choler; which is an Humour that maketh men active, earnest, full of alacritie, and stirring, if it be not stopped. But if it be stopped, and cannot have his way, it becometh adust, and thereby maligne and venomous. So Ambitious Men, if they find the way open for their rising, and still get forward, they are rather busie then dangerous; but if they be check't in their desires, they become secretly discontent, and looke upon men and matters with an evill eye, and are best pleased, when things goe backward; which is the worst propertie in a servant of a Prince or State. Therefore it is good for Princes, if they use Ambitious men, to handle it so as they be still progressive and not retrograde: which because it cannot be without inconvenience, it is good not to use such natures at all. For if they rise not with their service, they will take order to make their service fall with them. But since we have said it were good not to use men of Ambitious Natures, except it be upon necessitie, it is fit we speake in what cases, they are of necessitie. Good commanders in the warres must be taken, be they never so Ambitious: for the use of their service dispenseth with the rest; and to take a soldier without Ambition is to pull off his spurres. There is also great use of Ambitious Men in being skreenes to Princes in matters of danger and envie: for no man will take that part, except he be like a seel'd dove, that mounts and mounts because he cannot see about him. There is use also of Ambitious Men in pulling downe the greatnesse of any subject that over-tops: as Tiberius used Macro in the pulling down of

Sejanus. Since therefore they must be used in such cases, there resteth to speake how they are to be brideled, that they may be lesse dangerous. There is lesse danger of them, if they be of meane birth, then if they be Noble: and if they be rather harsh of nature, then gracious and popular: and if they be rather new raised, then growne cunning and fortified in their greatnesse. It is counted by some a weaknesse in Princes to have favorites: but it is of all others the best remedy against Ambitious Great-Ones. For when the way of pleasuring and displeasuring lieth by the favourite, it is impossible any other should be over-great. Another meanes to curbe them is to ballance them by others as proud as they. But then there must be some middle Counsellours to keep things steady: for without that ballast, the ship will roule too much. At the least, a Prince may animate and inure some meaner persons, to be as it were scourges to Ambitious Men. As for the having of them obnoxious to ruine, if they be of fearefull natures, it may doe well: but if they bee stout and daring, it may precipitate their designes, and prove dangerous. As for the pulling of them downe, if the affaires require it, and that it may not be done with safety suddainly, the onely way is the enterchange continually of favours and disgraces; whereby they may not know what to expect, and be as it were in a wood. Of Ambitions, it is lesse harmefull, the Ambition to prevaile in great things, then that other, to appeare in every thing; for that breeds confusion, and marres businesse. But yet it is lesse danger to have an Ambitious Man stirring in businesse, then great in dependances. He that seeketh to be eminent amongst able men hath a great taske; but that is ever good for the Publique. But he that plots to be the onely figure amongst ciphars is the decay of an whole age. Honour hath three things in it: the vantage ground to doe good; the approach to Kings and principall persons: and the raising of a man's owne fortunes. He that hath the best of these intentions, when he aspireth, is an honest man: and that Prince that can discerne of these intentions in another that aspireth, is a wise Prince. Generally, let Princes and States choose such Ministers as are more sensible of duty then of rising; and such as love businesse rather upon conscience then upon bravery: and let them discerne a busie nature from a willing minde.

❧ Of Masques and Triumphs.

THESE things are but Toyes, to come amongst such serious observations. But yet, since Princes will have such things, it is better they should be graced with elegancy then daubed with cost. Dancing to Song is a thing of great state and pleasure. I understand it, that the song be in Quire, placed aloft, and accompanied with some broken Musicke: and the ditty fitted to the device. Acting in Song, especially in Dialogues, hath an extreme good grace: I say Acting, not Dancing (for that is a meane and vulgar thing); and the Voices of the Dialogue would be strong and manly, (a base and a tenour; no treble); and the Ditty high and tragicall; not nice or dainty. Severall Quires, placed one over against another, and taking the voice by catches, Antheme wise, give great pleasure. Turning Dances into Figure is a childish curiosity. And generally, let it be noted, that those things which I here set downe are such as doe naturally take the sense, and not respect petty wonderments. It is true, the Alterations of Scenes, so it be quietly and without noise, are things of great beauty and pleasure: for they feed and relieve the eye, before it be full of the same object. Let the Scenes abound with Light, specially coloured and varied: and let the masquers, or any other, that are to come down from the Scene, have some motions upon the Scene it selfe before their comming down: for it drawes the eye strangely, & makes it with great pleasure to desire to see that it cannot perfectly discerne. Let the Songs be Loud and Cheerefull, and not Chirpings or Pulings. Let the Musicke likewise be Sharpe and Loud, and well placed. The Colours that shew best by candlelight are white, carnation, and a kinde of sea-water-greene; and Oes, or Spangs, as they are of no great cost, so they are of most glory. As for rich Embroidery, it is lost and not discerned. Let the Sutes of the Masquers be gracefull, and such as become the person when the vizars are off: not after examples of knowne attires; Turks, soldiers, mariners, and the like. Let Antimasques not be long; they have been commonly of fooles, satyres, baboones, wilde-men, antiques, beasts, sprites, witches, Ethiopes, pigmies, turquets, nimphs, rusticks, Cupids, statuas moving, and the like. As for Angels, it is not comicall enough to put them in antimasques; and any thing that is hideous, as devils, giants, is on the other side as unfit. But chiefly, let the Musicke of them be recreative and with some strange changes. Some sweet Odours suddenly comming forth, without any drops falling, are, in such a company as there is steame and heate, things of great pleasure & refreshment. Double Masques, one of men, another of ladies, addeth state and variety. But all is nothing except the roome be kept cleare and neat.

For Justs, and Tourneys, and Barriers; the glories of them are chiefly in the chariots, wherein the challengers make their entry; especially if they be drawne with strange beasts; as lions, beares, cammels, and the like: or in the devices of their entrance; or in the bravery of their liveries; or in the goodly furniture of their horses, and armour. But enough of these Toyes.

❧ Of Nature in Men.

NATURE is often hidden; sometimes overcome; seldome extinguished. Force maketh Nature more violent in the returne: doctrine and discourse maketh Nature lesse importune: but custome onely doth alter and subdue Nature. Hee that seeketh victory over his Nature, let him not set himselfe too great nor too small tasks; for the first will make him dejected by often faylings; and the second will make him a small proceeder, though by often prevailings. And at the first let him practise with helps, as swimmers doe with bladders or rushes: but after a time let him practise with disadvantages, as dancers doe with thick shooes. For it breeds great perfection, if the practise be harder then the use. Where Nature is mighty, and therefore the victory hard, the degrees had need be; first to stay and arrest Nature in time; like to him, that would say over the foure and twenty letters when he was angry: then to goe lesse in quantity; as if one should in forbearing wine, come from drinking healths to a draught at a meale: and lastly, to discontinue altogether. But if a man have the fortitude and resolution to enfranchise himselfe at once, that is the best;

Optimus ille animi vindex lædentia pectus
Vincula qui rupit, dedoluitque semel.

Neither is the ancient rule amisse, to bend Nature as a wand to a contrary extreme, whereby to set it right; understanding it, where the contrary extreme is no vice. Let not a man force a habit upon himselfe with a perpetuall continuance, but with some intermission. For both the pause reinforceth the new onset; and if a man that is not perfect be ever in practise, he shall as well practise his errours as his abilities; and induce one habite of both: and there is no meanes to helpe this but by seasonable intermissions. But let not a man trust his victorie over his Nature too farre; for Nature will lay buried a great time, and yet revive upon the occasion or temptation. Like as it was with Aesope's Damosell, turned from a Catt to a Woman; who sate very demurely at the board's end, till a Mouse ranne before her. Therefore let a man either avoid the occasion altogether; or put himselfe often to it, that hee may be little moved with it. A man's Nature is best perceived in privatenesse, for there is no affectation; in passion, for that putteth a man out of his precepts; and in a new case or experiment, for there custome leaveth him. They are happie men whose Natures sort with their vocations; otherwise they may say, *multum incola fuit anima mea:* when they converse in those things, they doe not affect. In studies, whatsoever a man commandeth upon himselfe, let him set houres for it: but whatsoever is agreeable to his Nature, let him take no care for any set times: for his thoughts will flie to it of themselves; so as the spaces of other businesse or studies will suffice. A man's Nature runnes either to herbes or weeds; therefore let him seasonably water the one, and destroy the other.

❧ Of Custome and Education.

MEN'S Thoughts are much according to their inclination: their Discourse & Speeches according to their learning and infused opinions; but their Deeds are after as they have beene Accustomed. And therefore, as Macciavel well noteth (though in an evill favoured instance), there is no trusting to the force of Nature nor to the bravery of words, except it be corroborate by Custome. His instance is, that for the atchieving of a desperate conspiracie, a man should not rest upon the fiercenesse of any man's nature, or his resolute undertakings; but take such an one as hath had his hands formerly in bloud. But Macciavel knew not of a Friar Clement, nor a Ravillac, nor a Jaureguy, nor a Baltazar Gerard: yet his rule holdeth still that Nature, nor the engagement of words, are not so forcible as Custome. Onely superstition is now so well advanced, that men of the first bloud are as firme as butchers by occupation: and votary resolution is made equipollent to Custome, even in matter of bloud. In other things the predominancy of Custome is every where visible; in so much as a man would wonder to heare men professe, protest, engage, give great words, and then doe just as they have done before: as if they were dead images, and engines moved onely by the wheeles of Custome. We see also the raigne or tyrannie of Custome, what it is. The Indians (I meane the sect of their wise men) lay themselves quietly upon a stacke of wood, and so sacrifice themselves by fire. Nay the wives strive to be burned with the corpses of their husbands. The lads of Sparta, of Ancient Time, were wont to be scourged upon the altar of Diana, without so much as queching. I remember in the beginning of Queene Elizabeth's time of England, an Irish Rebell condemned, put up a petition to the Deputie, that he might be hanged in a with, and not in an halter, because it had beene so used with former Rebels. There be monkes in Russia, for penance, that will sit a whole night in a vessell of water, till they be ingaged with hard ice. Many examples may be put of the force of Custome, both upon minde and body. Therefore, since Custome is the principall magistrate of man's life, let men by all meanes endevour to obtaine good Customes. Certainly Custome is most perfect when it beginneth in young yeares: this we call Education; which is, in effect, but an Early Custome. So we see, in languages the tongue is more pliant to all expressions and sounds, the joints are more supple to all feats of activitie and motions, in youth then afterwards. For it is true that late learners cannot so well take the plie; except it be in some mindes that have not suffered themselves to fixe, but have kept themselves open and prepared to receive continuall amendment, which is exceeding rare. But if the force of Custome simple and separate be great, the force of Custome copulate and conjoyned and collegiate is far greater. For there example teacheth, company comforteth, emulation quickeneth, glory raiseth: so as in such places the force of Custome is in his exaltation. Certainly the great multiplication of vertues upon humane nature resteth upon societies well ordained and disciplined. For commonwealths and good governments doe nourish Vertue growne, but doe not much mende the seeds. But the misery is, that the most effectuall Meanes are now applied to the Ends least to be desired.

❧ Of Fortune.

IT cannot be denied, but outward accidents conduce much to Fortune: favour, opportunitie, death of others, occasion fitting vertue. But chiefly, the mould of a man's Fortune is in his owne hands. *Faber quisque fortunæ suæ;* saith the poet. And the most frequent of externall causes is, that the Folly of one man is the Fortune of another. For no man prospers so suddenly as by others' errours. *Serpens nisi serpentem comederit non fit draco.* Overt, and apparent vertues bring forth praise; but there be secret and hidden vertues, that bring forth Fortune, certaine deliveries of a man's selfe, which have no name. The Spanish name, *Desemboltura*, partly expresseth them: when there be not stonds nor restivenesse in a man's nature; but that the wheeles of his minde keepe way with the wheeles of his Fortune. For so Livie (after he had described Cato Major, in these words; *In illo viro tantum robur corporis & animi fuit, ut quocunque loco natus esset, fortunam sibi facturus videretur*); falleth upon that, that he had *versatile ingenium*. Therfore, if a man looke sharply, and attentively, he shall see Fortune: for though shee be blinde, yet shee is not invisible. The way of Fortune is like the Milken Way in the skie; which is a meeting or knot of a number of small stars; not seene asunder, but giving light together. So are there a number of little and scarce discerned vertues, or rather faculties and customes, that make men Fortunate. The Italians note some of them, such as a man would little thinke. When they speake of one that cannot doe amisse, they will throw in into his other conditions, that he hath *Poco di matto*. And certainly, there be not two more fortunate properties, then to have a little of the foole, and not too much of the honest. Therefore, extreme lovers of their countrey or masters were never Fortunate, neither can they be. For when a man placeth his thoughts without himselfe, he goeth not his owne way. An hastie Fortune maketh an enterpriser & remover, (the French hath it better; *entreprenant* or *remuant*) but the exercised Fortune maketh the able man. Fortune is to be honoured and respected, and it bee but for her daughters, Confidence and Reputation. For those two felicitie breedeth: the first within a man's selfe, the latter in others towards him. All wise men, to decline the envy of their owne vertues, use to ascribe them to Providence and Fortune; for so they may the better assume them: and besides, it is greatnesse in a man to be the care of the higher powers. So Cæsar said to the pilot in the tempest, *Cæsarem portas, & fortunam ejus*. So Sylla chose the name of *Felix*, and not of *Magnus*. And it hath beene noted, that those that ascribe openly too much to their owne wisdome and policie end Infortunate. It is written, that Timotheus the Athenian, after he had, in the account he gave to the State of his Government, often interlaced this speech, *and in this Fortune had no part*, never prospered in any thing he undertooke afterwards. Certainly there be, whose Fortunes are like Homer's verses, that have a slide and easinesse, more then the verses of other poets: as Plutarch saith of Timoleon's Fortune, in respect of that of Agesilaus or Epaminondas. And that this should be, no doubt it is much in a man's selfe.

❧ Of Usurie.

MANY have made wittie invectives against Usurie. They say that it is pitie the Devill should have God's part, which is the Tithe. That the Usurer is the greatest Sabbath breaker, because his plough goeth every Sunday. That the Usurer is the droane that Virgil speaketh of:

Ignavum fucos pecus a præsepibus arcent.

That the Usurer breaketh the first law that was made for mankinde after the fall; which was, *In sudore vultus tui comedes panem tuum;* not *in sudore vultus alieni.* That Usurers should have orange-tawney bonnets, because they doe judaize. That it is against nature for money to beget money; and the like. I say this onely, that Usury is a *concessum propter duritiem cordis:* for since there must be borrowing and lending, and men are so hard of heart as they will not lend freely, Usury must be permitted. Some others have made suspicious and cunning propositions, of bankes, discovery of men's estates, and other inventions. But few have spoken of Usury usefully. It is good to set before us the Incommodities and Commodities of Usury; that the good may be either weighed out or culled out; and warily to provide, that while we make forth to that which is better, we meet not with that which is worse.

The Discommodities of Usury are: First, that it makes fewer merchants. For were it not for this lazie trade of Usury, money would not lie still, but would in great part be imployed upon merchandizing; which is the *vena porta* of wealth in a State. The second, that it makes poore merchants. For as a farmer cannot husband his ground so well if he sit at a great rent; so the merchant cannot drive his trade so well, if he sit at great Usury. The third is incident to the other two; and that is, the decay of Customes of Kings or States, which ebbe or flow with merchandizing. The fourth, that it bringeth the treasure of a Realme or State into a few hands. For the Usurer being at certainties, and others at uncertainties, at the end of the game most of the money will be in the boxe; and ever a State flourisheth, when wealth is more equally spread. The fifth, that it beats downe the price of land; for the employment of money is chiefly either merchandizing or purchasing; and Usury waylayes both. The sixth, that it doth dull and dampe all industries, improvements, and new inventions, wherin money would be stirring, if it were not for this slugge. The last, that it is the canker and ruine of many men's Estates; which in processe of time breeds a publike povertie.

On the other side, the Commodities of Usury are, first, that howsoever Usury in some respect hindereth merchandizing, yet in some other it advanceth it: for it is certain that the greatest part of trade is driven by young merchants, upon borrowing at interest; so as if the Usurer either call in or keepe backe his money, there will ensue presently a great stand of trade. The second is, that were it not for this easie borrowing upon interest, men's necessities would draw upon them a most sudden undoing; in that they would be forced to sell their meanes (be it lands or goods) farre under foot; and so, whereas Usury doth but gnaw upon them, bad markets would swallow them quite up. As for mortgaging or pawning, it will little mend the matter; for either men will not take pawnes without Use; or if they doe, they will looke precisely for the forfeiture. I remember a cruell moneyed man in the country, that would say; The Devill take this Usury, it keepes us from forfeitures of mortgages and bonds. The third and last is, that it is a vanitie to conceive that there would be ordinary Borrowing without profit; and it is impossible to conceive the number of inconveniences that will ensue, if Borrowing be cramped. Therefore, to speake of the abolishing of Usury is idle. All States have ever had it, in one kinde or rate, or other. So as that opinion must be sent to Utopia.

To speake now, of the Reformation and Reiglement of Usury; how the Discommodities of it may be best avoided, and the Commodities retained. It appeares by the ballance of Commodities and Discommodities of Usury, two things are to be reconciled. The one, that the tooth of Usurie be grinded, that it bite not too much: the other, that there bee left open a meanes to invite moneyed men to lend to the merchants for the continuing and quickning of Trade. This cannot be done, except you introduce two severall sorts of Usury; a lesse, and a greater. For if you reduce Usury to one low rate, it will ease the common borrower, but the merchant wil be to seeke for money. And it is to be noted, that the trade of Merchandize, being the most lucrative, may beare Usury at a good rate; other contracts not so.

To serve both intentions, the way would be briefly thus. That there be two rates of Usury, the one free, and generall for all; the other under licence only, to certaine persons and in certaine places of merchandizing. First therefore, let Usury in generall be reduced to five in the hundred; and let that rate be proclaimed to be free and current; and let the State shut it selfe out to take any penalty for the same. This will preserve borrowing from any generall stop or drinesse. This will ease infinite borrowers in the countrie. This will, in good part, raise the price of land, because land purchased at sixteene yeares' purchase will yeeld six in the hundred, and somewhat more, whereas this rate of interest yeelds but five. This, by like reason, will encourage and edge industrious and profitable improvements; because many will rather venture in that kinde then take five in the hundred, especially having beene used to greater profit. Secondly, let there be certaine persons licensed to lend to knowne merchants upon Usury at a higher rate; and let it be with the cautions following. Let the rate be, even with the merchant himselfe, somewhat more easie then that he used formerly to pay; for by that meanes all borrowers shall have some ease by this reformation, be he merchant, or whosoever. Let it be no Banke or Common Stocke, but every man be master of his owne money: Not that I altogether mislike Banks, but they will hardly be brooked, in regard of certain suspicions. Let the State be answered some small matter for the licence, and the rest left to the lender: for if the abatement be but small, it will no whit discourage the lender. For he, for example, that tooke before ten or nine in the hundred, wil sooner descend to eight in the hundred then give over his trade of Usury; and goe from certaine gaines to gaines of hazard. Let these licenced lenders be in number indefinite, but restrained to certaine principall cities and townes of merchandizing; for then they will be hardly able to colour other men's moneyes in the country: so as the Licence of Nine will not sucke away the current Rate of Five; for no man will lend his moneyes farre off, nor put them into unknown hands.

If it be objected, that this doth in a sort authorize Usury, which before was in some places but permissive; the answer is, that it is better to mitigate Usury by Declaration, then to suffer it to rage by Connivence.

Of Youth and Age.

A MAN that is young in Yeares may be old in Houres, if he have lost no time. But that happeneth rarely. Generally, Youth is like the first cogitations, not so wise as the second. For there is a Youth in Thoughts as well as in Ages. And yet the invention of Young Men is more lively, then that of Old; and imaginations streame into their mindes better and, as it were, more divinely. Natures that have much heat and great and violent desires and perturbations are not ripe for action, till they have passed the meridian of their yeares: as it was with Julius Cæsar, and Septimius Severus. Of the latter of whom it is said; *Juventutem egit erroribus, imo furoribus, plenam*. And yet he was the ablest Emperour, almost, of all the list. But reposed natures may doe well in Youth. As it is seene in Augustus Cæsar, Cosmus Duke of Florence, Gaston de Fois, and others. On the other side, heate and vivacity in Age is an excellent composition for businesse. Young Men are fitter to invent then to judge; fitter for execution then for counsell; and fitter for new Projects then for setled businesse. For the experience of Age, in things that fall within the compasse of it, directeth them; but in new things, abuseth them.

The errours of Young Men are the ruine of businesse; but the errours of Aged Men amount but to this; that more might have beene done, or sooner. Young Men, in the conduct and mannage of actions, embrace more then they can hold; stirre more then they can quiet; fly to the end, without consideration of the meanes and degrees; pursue some few principles which they have chanced upon absurdly; care not to innovate, which draws unknowne inconveniences; use extreme remedies at first; and that which doubleth all errours, will not acknowledge or retract them; like an unready horse, that will neither stop nor turne. Men of Age object too much, consult too long, adventure too little, repent too soone, and seldome drive businesse home to the full period; but content themselves with a mediocrity of successe. Certainly it is good to compound employments of both; for that will be good for the present, because the vertues of either Age may correct the defects of both; and good for succession, that Young Men may be learners, while Men in Age are actours: and lastly, good for externe accidents, because authority followeth Old Men, and favour and popularity Youth. But for the morall part, perhaps Youth will have the preheminence, as Age hath for the politique. A certaine Rabbine, upon the text, *Your young men shall see visions, and your old men shall dreame dreames*, inferreth that Young Men are admitted nearer to God then Old; because vision is a clearer revelation then a dreame. And certainly, the more a man drinketh of the world, the more it intoxicateth; and Age doth profit rather in the powers of understanding, then in the vertues of the will and affections. There be some have an overearly ripenesse in their yeares, which fadeth betimes. These are, first, such as have brittle wits, the edge whereof is soone turned; such as was Hermogenes the Rhetorician, whose books are exceeding subtill; who afterwards waxed stupid. A second sort is of those that have some naturall dispositions which have better grace in Youth then in Age: such as is a fluent and luxuriant speech; which becomes Youth well, but not Age: so Tully saith of Hortensius; *Idem manebat, neque idem decebat.* The third is of such as take too high a straine at the first, and are magnanimous more then tract of yeares can uphold. As was Scipio Affricanus, of whom Livy saith in effect; *Ultima primis cedebant.*

❧ Of Beauty.

VERTUE is like a rich stone, best plaine set: and surely, Vertue is best in a body that is comely, though not of delicate features: and that hath rather dignity of presence, then Beauty of aspect. Neither is it almost seene, that very Beautifull Persons are otherwise of great Vertue; as if Nature were rather busie not to erre, then in labour to produce excellency. And therefore, they prove accomplished, but not of great spirit; and study rather behaviour, then Vertue. But this holds not alwaies; for Augustus Cæsar, Titus Vespasianus, Philip le Belle of France, Edward the Fourth of England, Alcibiades of Athens, Ismael the Sophy of Persia, were all high and great spirits; and yet the most Beautifull Men of their times. In Beauty, that of favour is more then that of colour, and that of decent and gracious motion more then that of favour. That is the best part of Beauty, which a picture cannot expresse; no nor the first sight of the life. There is no excellent Beauty that hath not some strangenesse in the proportion. A man cannot tell, whether Apelles or Albert Durer, were the more trifler: whereof the one would make a Personage by geometricall proportions: the other, by taking the best parts out of divers Faces to make one excellent. Such Personages, I thinke, would please no body but the Painter that made them. Not but I thinke a Painter may make a better Face then ever was; but he must doe it by a kinde of felicity, (as a Musician that maketh an excellent ayre in Musicke) and not by rule. A man shall see faces, that if you examine them part by part, you shall finde never a good; and yet all together doe well. If it be true, that the principall part of Beauty is in decent motion, certainly it is no marvaile though Persons in Yeares seeme many times more amiable; *pulchrorum autumnus pulcher:* for no Youth can be comely but by pardon, & considering the Youth as to make up the comelinesse. Beauty is as summer-fruits, which are easie to corrupt, & cannot last: and for the most part it makes a dissolute Youth and an Age a little out of countenance: but yet certainly againe, if it light well, it maketh Vertues shine and Vices blush.

❧ Of Deformity.

DEFORMED persons are commonly even with Nature: for as Nature hath done ill by them, so doe they by Nature: being for the most part (as the Scripture saith), *void of naturall affection;* and so they have their revenge of Nature. Certainly there is a consent between the body and the minde; and where Nature erreth in the one, she ventureth in the other. *Ubi peccat in uno, periclitatur in altero.* But because there is in man an election touching the frame of his minde, and a necessity in the frame of his body, the starres of naturall inclination, are sometimes obscured by the sun of Discipline and Vertue. Therefore it is good to consider of Deformity, not as a signe, which is more deceivable; but as a cause, which seldome faileth of the effect. Whosoever hath any thing fixed in his person that doth enduce contempt, hath also a perpetuall spurre in himselfe to rescue & deliver himselfe from scorne: therefore all Deformed Persons are extreme bold. First, as in their own defence, as being exposed to scorn; but in processe of time, by a generall habit. Also it stirreth in them industry, and especially of this kinde, to watch and observe the weaknesse of others, that they may have somewhat to repay. Againe, in their superiours, it quencheth jealousie towards them, as persons that they think they may at pleasure despise: and it layeth their competitours and emulatours asleepe; as never beleeving they should be in possibility of advancement till they see them in possession. So that upon the matter, in a great wit, Deformity is an advantage to rising. Kings in Ancient Times (and at this present in some countries), were wont to put great trust in Eunuchs; because they, that are envious towards all are more obnoxious and officious towards one. But yet their trust towards them hath rather beene as to good Spialls and good Whisperers; then good Magistrates and Officers. And much like is the reason of Deformed Persons. Still the ground is, they will, if they be of spirit, seeke to free themselves from scorne; which must be either by vertue or malice: and therefore let it not be marvelled if sometimes they prove excellent persons; as was Agesilaus, Zanger the sonne of Solyman, Æsope, Gasca, President of Peru; & Socrates may goe likewise amongst them; with others.

❧ Of Building.

HOUSES are built to live in, and not to looke on: therefore let use bee preferred before uniformitie; except where both may be had. Leave the goodly fabrickes of Houses, for beautie only, to the enchanted pallaces of the poets: who build them with small cost. Hee that builds a faire House upon an ill Seat, committeth himselfe to prison. Neither doe I reckon it an ill Seat, only, where the aire is unwholesome; but likewise where the aire is unequall; as you shall see many fine Seats set upon a knap of ground, environed with higher hilles round about it: whereby the heat of the Sunne is pent in, and the Wind gathereth as in troughes; so as you shall have, and that suddenly, as great diversitie of heat and cold as if you dwelt in severall places. Neither is it ill Aire onely that maketh an ill Seat, but ill Wayes, ill Markets; and, if you will consult with Momus, ill Neighbours. I speake not of many more: want of Water; want of Wood, Shade, and Shelter; want of Fruitfulnesse, and mixture of Grounds of severall natures; want of Prospect; want of Levell Grounds; want of Places at some neare distance for sports of Hunting, Hauking, and Races; too neare the Sea, too remote; having the commoditie of Navigable Rivers, or the discommoditie of their overflowing; too farre off from great Cities, which may hinder businesse; or too neare them, which lurcheth all provisions, and maketh every thing deare; where a man hath a great Living laid together, and where he is scanted: all which, as it is impossible perhaps to finde together, so it is good to know them, and thinke of them, that a man may take as many as he can: and if he have severall Dwellings, that he sort them so, that what hee wanteth in the one hee may finde in the other. Lucullus answered Pompey well; who, when hee saw his stately galleries, and roomes, so large and lightsome, in one of his Houses, said; *Surely an excellent place for Summer, but how doe you in Winter?* Lucullus answered; *Why doe you not think me as wise as some fowle are, that ever change their aboad towards the Winter?*

To passe from the Seat, to the House it selfe; we will doe as Cicero doth, in the oratour's art; who writes bookes *De Oratore*, and a booke he entitles *Orator:* whereof the former delivers the precepts of the art, and the latter the perfection. We will therefore describe a princely Pallace, making a briefe modell thereof. For it is strange to see, now in Europe, such huge buildings as the Vatican and Escuriall and some others be, and yet scarce a very faire roome in them.

First therefore, I say, you cannot have a perfect Pallace, except you have two severall sides; a side for the Banquet as is spoken of in the booke of Hester; and a side for the Houshold: the one for feasts and triumphs, and the other for dwelling. I understand both these sides to be not onely returnes but parts of the front; and to be uniforme without, though severally partitioned within; and to be on both sides of a great and stately Tower, in the middest of the front; that as it were, joyneth them together on either hand. I would have on the side of the Banquet, in front, one only goodly roome above staires, of some fortie foot high; and under it a roome for a dressing or preparing place at times of Triumphs. On the other side, which is the Household side, I wish it divided at the first into a Hall, and a Chappell (with a partition betweene); both of good state and bignesse: and those not to goe all the length, but to have at the further end, a Winter and a Summer Parler, both faire. And under these roomes, a faire and large Cellar suncke under ground: and likewise, some privie Kitchins, with Butteries and Pantries, and the like. As for the Tower, I would have it two stories, of eighteene foot high a peece, above the two wings; and a goodly Leads upon the top, railed with Statuas interposed; and the same Tower to bee divided into roomes, as shall be thought fit. The Staires likewise, to the upper roomes, let them bee upon a faire open Newell and finely raild in, with Images of wood, cast into a brasse colour: and a very faire Landing Place at the top. But this to be, if you doe not point any of the lower roomes for a dining place of servants. For otherwise you shall have the servants' dinner after your owne: for the steame of it will come up as in a tunnell. And so much for the Front. Only, I understand the height of the first staires to be sixteene foot, which is the height of the lower roome.

Beyond this Front is there to be a faire Court, but three sides of it of a farre lower building then the Front. And in all the foure corners of that Court, faire staire cases, cast into Turrets on the outside, and not within the row of Buildings themselves. But those Towers are not to be of the height of the Front; but rather proportionable to the lower building. Let the Court not be paved, for that striketh up a great heat in Summer and much cold in Winter. But onely some side alleys, with a crosse, and the quarters to graze, being kept shorne, but not too neare shorne. The row of Returne, on the Banquet side, let it be all stately Galleries; in which Galleries let there be three, or five, fine Cupolas in the length of it, placed at equall distance: and fine coloured Windowes of severall workes. On the household side, Chambers of Presence, & ordinary entertainments, with some Bedchambers; and let all three sides be a double House, without thorow lights on the sides, that you may have roomes from the Sunne, both for fore-noone and after-noone. Cast it also, that you may have roomes, both for Summer, and Winter: shadie for Summer, and warme for Winter. You shall have sometimes faire Houses so full of glasse that one cannot tell where to become to be out of the Sunne or cold. For inbowed Windowes, I hold them of good use; (in cities indeed, upright doe better, in respect of the uniformitie towards the street); for they bee prettie retiring places for conference; and besides, they keepe both the wind and sunne off: for that which would strike almost thorow the Roome, doth scarce passe the Window. But let them be but few, foure in the Court, on the sides onely.

Beyond this Court, let there be an inward Court of the same square and height; which is to be environed, with the Garden, on all sides: and in the inside, cloistered on all sides, upon decent and beautifull arches, as high as the first Story. On the under Story, towards the Garden, let it be turned to a Grotta, or place of shade, or estivation. And onely have opening and Windowes towards the Garden; and be levell upon the floare, no whit sunke under ground, to avoid all dampishnesse. And let there be a Fountaine, or some faire worke of Statuas, in the middest of this Court; and to be paved as the other Court was. These buildings to be for privie Lodgings, on both sides; and the end for privie Galleries. Whereof you must fore-see that one of them be for an Infirmary, if the Prince or any speciall person should be sicke, with Chambers, Bed-chamber, Anticamera, and Recamera, joyning to it. This upon the second story. Upon the ground story, a faire Gallery, open, upon pillars: and upon the third story likewise, an open Gallery upon pillars, to take the prospect and freshnesse of the Garden. At both corners of the further side, by way of returne, let there be two delicate or rich Cabinets, daintily paved, richly hanged, glased with crystalline glasse, and a rich Cupola in the middest; and all other elegancie that may be thought upon. In the upper Gallery too, I wish that there may be, if the place will yeeld it, some Fountaines running in divers places from the wall, with some fine avoidances. And thus much for the modell of the Pallace: save that you must have, before you come to the front, three Courts. A greene Court plain, with a wall about it: a second Court of the same, but more garnished, with little turrets, or rather embellishments, upon the wall: and a third Court, to make a square with the front, but not to be built nor yet enclosed with a naked wall, but enclosed with Tarrasses, leaded aloft, and fairely garnished on the three sides; and cloistered on the inside with pillars, and not with arches below. As for Offices, let them stand at distance, with some low Galleries, to passe from them to the Pallace it selfe.

Of Gardens.

GOD Almightie first planted a Garden. And indeed it is the purest of humane pleasures. It is the greatest refreshment to the spirits of man; without which Buildings and Pallaces are but grosse handy-works: and a man shall ever see that when ages grow to civility and elegancie, men come to Build stately sooner then to Garden finely: as if Gardening were the greater perfection. I doe hold it, in the royall ordering of Gardens, there ought to be Gardens for all the moneths in the yeare: in which, severally, things of beautie may be then in season. For December, and January, and the latter part of November, you must take such things as are greene all Winter: holly; ivy; bayes; juniper; cipresse trees; eugh; pine-apple-trees; firre-trees; rose-mary; lavander; periwinckle, the white, the purple, and the blewe; germander; flagges; orenge-trees; limon-trees; and mirtles, if they be stooved; and sweet marjoram warme set. There followeth, for the latter part of January, and February, the mezerion tree, which then blossomes; crocus vernus, both the yellow, and the gray; prime-roses; anemones; the early tulippa; hiacynthus orientalis; chamaïris; frettellaria. For March, there come violets, specially the single blew, which are the earliest; the yellow daffadill; the dazie; the almond-tree in blossome; the peach-tree in blossome; the cornelian-tree in blossome; sweet-briar. In Aprill follow, the double white violet; the wall-flower; the stock-gilly-flower; the couslip; flower-delices, and lillies of all natures; rose-mary flowers; the tulippa; the double piony; the pale daffadill; the French honny-suckle; the cherry-tree in blossome; the dammasin, and plum-trees in blossome; the white-thorne in leafe; the lelacke tree. In May, and June, come pincks of all sorts, specially the blush pincke; roses of all kinds, except the muske, which comes later; hony-suckles; strawberries; buglosse; columbine; the French mary-gold; flos Africanus; cherry-tree in fruit; ribes; figges in fruit; raspes; vine flowers; lavender in flowers; the sweet satyrian, with the white flower; herba muscaria; lilium convallium; the apple-tree in blossome. In July, come gilly-flowers of all varieties; muske roses; the lime-tree in blossome; early peares, and plummes in fruit; ginnitings; quadlins. In August, come plummes of all sorts in fruit; peares; apricockes; berberies; filberds; muske-melons; monks hoods of all colours. In September, come grapes; apples; poppies of all colours; peaches; melocotones; nectarines; cornelians; wardens; quinces. In October, and the beginning of November, come services; medlars; bullises; roses cut or removed to come late; hollyokes; and such like. These particulars are for the climate of London; but my meaning is perceived, that you may have *ver perpetuum*, as the place affords.

And because the breath of Flowers, is farre sweeter in the aire (where it comes and goes, like the warbling of musick) then in the hand, therfore nothing is more fit for that delight then to know what be the Flowers and Plants that doe best perfume the aire. Roses, damask and red, are fast flowers of their smels; so that you may walke by a whole row of them and finde nothing of their sweetnesse; yea though it be in a morning's dew. Bayes likewise yeeld no smell as they grow. Rosemary little; nor sweet-marjoram. That which above all others yeelds the sweetest smell in the aire is the violet; specially the white-double-violet, which comes twice a yeare; about the middle of Aprill, and about Bartholomew-tide. Next to that is the muske-rose. Then the strawberry-leaves dying, which [yeeld] a most excellent cordiall smell. Then the flower of the vines; it is a little dust, like the dust of a bent, which growes upon the cluster, in the first comming forth. Then sweet briar. Then wall-flowers, which are very delightfull to be set under a parler or lower chamber window. Then pincks and gilly-flowers, specially the matted pinck and clove gilly-flower. Then the flowers of the lime tree. Then the hony-suckles, so they be somewhat a farre off. Of beane flowers I speake not, because they are field flowers. But those which perfume the aire most delightfully, not passed by as the rest, but being troden upon and crushed, are three: that is, burnet, wilde-time, and water-mints. Therefore, you are to set whole allies of them, to have the pleasure when you walke or tread.

For Gardens (speaking of those which are indeed Prince-like, as we have done of Buildings), the contents ought not well to be under thirty acres of ground, and to be divided into three parts: a Greene in the entrance; a Heath or Desart in the going forth; and the Maine Garden in the midst; besides Alleys on both sides. And I like well that foure acres of ground be assigned to the Greene; six to the Heath; foure and foure to either Side; and twelve to the Maine Garden. The Greene hath two pleasures; the one because nothing is more pleasant to the eye then greene grasse kept finely shorne; the other, because it will give you a faire Alley in the midst, by which you may go in front upon a stately Hedge, which is to inclose the Garden. But, because the alley will be long, and, in great heat of the yeare or day, you ought not to buy the shade in the Garden by going in the sunne thorow the Greene, therefore you are, of either side the Greene, to plant a covert Alley, upon Carpenter's worke, about twelve foot in height, by which you may goe in shade into the Garden. As for the making of Knots, or Figures, with divers coloured Earths, that they may lie under the windowes of the House, on that side which the Garden stands, they be but Toyes: you may see as good sights many times, in Tarts. The Garden is best to be square; incompassed on all the foure sides with a stately arched Hedge. The Arches to be upon Pillars of carpenter's worke, of some ten foot high, and six foot broad: and the Spaces between, of the same dimension, with the Breadth of the Arch. Over the Arches let there bee an entire Hedge, of some foure foot high, framed also upon carpenter's Worke: and upon the upper Hedge, over every Arch, a little Turret, with a Belly, enough to receive a cage of Birds: and over every Space, betweene the Arches, some other little Figure, with broad plates of round coloured Glasse, gilt, for the Sunne to play upon. But this Hedge I entend to be raised upon a Bancke not steepe, but gently slope, of some six foot, set all with Flowers. Also I understand, that this Square of the Garden should not be the whole breadth of the ground, but to leave, on either side, ground enough for diversity of Side Alleys: unto which the two Covert Alleys of the Greene may deliver you. But there must be no Alleys with Hedges at either End of this great Inclosure: not at the hither End, for letting your prospect upon this faire Hedge from the Greene; nor at the Further End, for letting your prospect from the Hedge through the Arches upon the Heath.

For the ordering of the ground, within the great Hedge, I leave it to variety of device; advising neverthelesse, that whatsoever forme you cast it into, first it be not too busie, or full of Worke. Wherein I, for my part, doe not like Images cut out in Juniper, or other Garden stuffe: they be for children. Little low Hedges, round, like welts, with some pretty Pyramides, I like well: and in some places, faire Columnes upon frames of carpenter's worke. I would also have the Alleys spacious and faire. You may have closer Alleys upon the Side Grounds, but none in the Maine Garden. I wish also, in the very middle, a faire Mount, with three ascents, and alleys, enough for foure to walke a breast; which I would have to be perfect circles, without any bulwarkes or imbosments; and the whole Mount, to be thirty foot high; and some fine Banquetting House, with some Chimneys neatly cast, and without too much Glasse.

For Fountaines, they are a great beauty and refreshment; but Pooles marre all, and make the Garden unwholsome, and full of flies and frogs. Fountaines I intend to be of two natures: the one, that Sprinckleth or Spouteth Water; the other a faire Receipt of Water, of some thirty or forty foot square, but without fish, or slime, or mud. For the first, the Ornaments of Images Gilt, or of Marble, which are in use, doe well: but the maine matter is, so to convey the Water as it never stay, either in the bowles or in the cesterne; that the water be never by rest discoloured, greene or red or the like; or gather any Mossinesse or Putrefaction. Besides that, it is to be cleansed every day by the hand. Also some Steps up to it, and some fine Pavement about it, doth well. As for the other kinde of Fountaine, which we may call a Bathing Poole, it may admit much curiosity and beauty; wherewith we will not trouble our selves: as, that the bottome be finely paved, and with Images: the sides likewise; and withall embellished with coloured Glasse, and such things of lustre; encompassed also, with fine Railes of low Statuas. But the maine point is the same which we mentioned in the former kinde of Fountaine; which is, that the water be in perpetuall motion, fed by a water higher then the Poole, and delivered into it by faire spouts, & then discharged away under ground by some equalitie of bores, that it stay little. And for fine devices, of arching Water without spilling, and making it rise in severall formes, (of Feathers, Drinking Glasses, Canopies and the like), they be pretty things to looke on, but nothing to health and sweetnesse.

For the Heath, which was the third part of our Plot, I wish it to be framed, as much as may be, to a Naturall wildnesse. Trees I would have none in it, but some Thickets, made onely of Sweet-Briar and Honny-suckle, & some wilde Vine amongst; and the ground set with Violets, Strawberries, and Prime-Roses. For these are sweet, and prosper in the shade. And these to be in the Heath, here and there, not in any order. I like also little Heaps, in the nature of Mole-hils (such as are in wilde Heaths), to be set, some with wilde Thyme; some with Pincks; some with Germander, that gives a good flower to the eye; some with Periwinckle; some with Violets; some with Strawberries; some with Couslips; some with Daisies; some with Red-Roses; some with Lilium Convallium; some with Sweet-Williams red; some with Beares-Foot; and the like low flowers, being withal sweet, and sightly. Part of which Heapes to be with Standards of little Bushes prickt upon their top, and part without. The Standards to be Roses; Juniper; Holly; Beare-berries (but here and there, because of the smell of their blossome); red Currans; Gooseberries; Rose-Mary; Bayes; Sweet-Briar; and such like. But these Standards to be kept with cutting, that they grow not out of course.

For the Side Grounds, you are to fill them with varietie of

Alleys, private, to give a full shade, some of them, wheresoever the Sun be. You are to frame some of them likewise for shelter, that when the wind blows sharpe, you may walke as in a Gallery. And those Alleys must be likewise hedged at both ends, to keepe out the Wind; and these Closer Alleys must bee ever finely gravelled, and no grasse, because of going wet. In many of these Alleys likewise, you are to set Fruit-Trees of all sorts; as well upon the walles, as in ranges. And this would be generally observed, that the Borders wherin you plant your Fruit-Trees, be faire & large, & low, & not steepe; and set with fine Flowers, but thin and sparingly, lest they deceive the Trees. At the end of both the Side Grounds, I would have a Mount of some pretty height, leaving the wall of the enclosure brest high, to looke abroad into the Fields.

For the Maine Garden, I doe not deny but there should be some faire Alleys, ranged on both sides, with Fruit Trees; and some pretty Tufts of Fruit Trees, & Arbours with Seats, set in some decent order; but these to be by no meanes set too thicke; but to leave the Maine Garden so as it be not close, but the aire open and free. For as for Shade, I would have you rest upon the Alleys of the Side Grounds, there to walke, if you be disposed, in the heat of the yeare or day; but to make account that the Maine Garden is for the more temperate parts of the yeare; and in the heat of Summer, for the Morning and the Evening, or over-cast Dayes.

For Aviaries I like them not, except they be of that largenesse as they may be Turffed, and have living Plants, and Bushes set in them; that the Birds may have more scope, & naturall neastling, and that no Foulenesse appeare in the Floare of the Aviary. So I have made a Platforme of a Princely Garden, partly by Precept, partly by Drawing, not a Modell, but some generall lines of it; and in this I have spared for no cost. But it is nothing for great Princes, that for the most part, taking advice with workmen, with no lesse cost, set their things together; and sometimes adde Statuas and such things, for State and Magnificence, but nothing to the true pleasure of a Garden.

❧ Of Negociating.

IT is generally better to deale by Speech, then by Letter; and by the mediation of a third then by a man's selfe. Letters are good, when a man would draw an answer by letter backe againe; or when it may serve for a man's justification, afterwards, to produce his owne letter; or where it may be danger to be interrupted, or heard by peeces. To deale in person is good, when a man's face breedeth regard, as commonly with inferiours; or in tender cases, where a man's eye, upon the countenance of him with whom he speaketh, may give him a Direction, how farre to goe: and generally, where a man will reserve to himselfe Libertie, either to disavow or to expound. In choice of Instruments, it is better to choose men of a plainer sort, that are like to doe that, that is committed to them, and to report back again faithfully the successe, then those that are cunning to contrive out of other men's businesse somewhat to grace themselves; and will helpe the matter in report for satisfaction sake. Use also such persons as affect the Businesse wherin they are employed; for that quickneth much; and such as are fit for the matter; as bold men for Expostulation, faire spoken men for Perswasion, craftie men for Enquiry and Observation, froward and absurd men for Businesse that doth not well beare out it selfe. Use also such as have beene luckie, and prevailed before in things wherein you have emploied them; for that breeds Confidence, and they will strive to maintaine their Prescription. It is better to sound a person with whom one Deales a farre off, then to fall upon the point at first; except you meane to surprize him by some short

Question. It is better Dealing with men in appetite, then with those that are where they would be. If a man Deale with another upon conditions, the start or first performance is all; which a man cannot reasonably demaund, except either the nature of the thing be such, which must goe before; or else a man can perswade the other partie that hee shall still need him in some other thing; or else that he be counted the honester man. All practise is to Discover, or to Worke. Men discover themselves in trust; in passion; at unawares; and of necessitie, when they would have somewhat done, and cannot finde an apt Pretext. If you would Worke any man, you must either know his Nature and Fashions, and so lead him; or his Ends, and so perswade him; or his Weaknesse and Disadvantages, and so awe him; or those that have Interest in him, and so governe him. In Dealing with cunning persons, we must ever consider their Ends, to interpret their Speeches; and it is good to say little to them, and that which they least looke for. In all Negociations of difficultie, a man may not looke to sowe and reape at once; but must prepare businesse, and so ripen it by degrees.

❧ Of Followers and Frends.

MOSTLY Followers are not to be liked; lest while a man maketh his traine longer, hee make his wings shorter. I reckon to bee costly, not them alone which charge the purse, but which are wearisome and importune in sutes. Ordinary Followers ought to challenge no higher conditions then countenance, recommendation, and protection from wrongs. Factious Followers are worse to be liked, which follow not upon affection to him with whom they range themselves, but upon discontentment conceived against some other: whereupon commonly ensueth that ill intelligence, that we many times see betweene great Personages. Likewise glorious Followers, who make themselves as trumpets of the commendation of those they follow, are full of inconvenience; for they taint businesse through want of secrecie; and they export honour from a man, and make him a returne in envie. There is a kinde of Followers likewise, which are dangerous, being indeed Espials; which enquire the secrets of the house, and beare tales of them to others. Yet such men, many times, are in great favour; for they are officious, and commonly exchange tales. The Following by certaine Estates of men, answerable to that which a Great Person himselfe professeth (as of Soldiers to him that hath been employed in the Warres, and the like), hath ever beene a thing civill, and well taken, even in Monarchies; so it be without too much pompe or popularitie. But the most honourable kinde of Following is to be followed, as one that apprehendeth to advance Vertue and Desert in all sorts of persons. And yet, where there is no eminent odds in Sufficience, it is better to take with the more passable, then with the more able. And besides, to speake truth, in base times active men are of more use then vertuous. It is true, that in Government, it is good to use men of one rancke equally: for to countenance some extraordinarily is to make them insolent, and the rest discontent; because they may claime a Due. But contrariwise, in favour, to use men with much difference and election is good; for it maketh the persons preferred more thankfull, and the rest more officious; because all is of Favour. It is good Discretion, not to make too much of any man, at the first; because one cannot hold out that Proportion. To be governed (as we call it) by one, is not safe: for it shewes Softnesse, and gives a freedome to Scandall and Disreputation: for those that would not censure or speake ill of a man immediately, will talke more boldly of those that are so great with them, and thereby wound their Honour. Yet to be distracted with many is worse; for it makes men to be of the last impression, and full of change. To take advice of some few frends is ever honourable; *for lookers on, many times see more then gamesters; and the vale best discovereth the hill.* There is little frendship in the world, and least of all betweene equals, which was wont to be magnified. That that is, is between Superiour and Inferiour, whose fortunes may comprehend, the one the other.

❧ Of Sutours.

MANY ill matters & projects are undertaken; and private Sutes do putrifie the publique good. Many good matters are undertaken with bad mindes; I meane not onely corrupt mindes, but craftie mindes, that intend not performance. Some embrace Sutes, which never meane to deale effectually in them; but if they see there may be life in the matter, by some other meane, they will be content to winne a thanke, or take a second reward, or at least to make use, in the meane time, of the Sutour's hopes. Some take hold of Sutes onely for an occasion to crosse some other; or to make an Information, whereof they could not otherwise have apt pretext; without care what become of the Sute when that turne is served; or generally, to make other men's businesse a kinde of entertainment to bring in their owne. Nay, some undertake Sutes, with a full purpose to let them fall; to the end, to gratifie the adverse partie or Competitour. Surely there is in some sort, a right in every Sute: either a right of equity, if it be a Sute of controversie; or a right of desert, if it be a Sute of petition. If affection lead a man to favour the wrong side in Justice, let him rather use his countenance to compound the matter then to carry it. If affection lead a man to favour the lesse worthy in desert, let him doe it without depraving or disabling the better deserver. In Sutes which a man doth not well understand, it is good to referre them to some frend of trust and judgement, that may report whether hee may deale in them with Honour: but let him chuse well his referendaries, for else he may be led by the nose. Sutours are so distasted with delayes and abuses, that plaine dealing in denying to deale in Sutes at first, and reporting the successe barely, and in challenging no more thanks then one hath deserved, is grown not onely honourable but also gracious. In Sutes of Favour, the first comming ought to take little place: so farre forth consideration may bee had of his Trust, that if intelligence of the matter could not otherwise have beene had but by him, advantage bee not taken of the note, but the Partie left to his other meanes; and, in some sort, recompenced for his discoverie. To be ignorant of the value of a Sute, is Simplicitie; as well as to be ignorant of the Right thereof is want of Conscience. Secrecie in Sutes is a great meane of obtaining; for voycing them to bee in forwardnesse may discourage some kinde of Sutours; but doth quicken and awake others. But Timing of the Sute is the Principall. Timing, I say, not onely in respect of the person that should grant it, but in respect of those which are like to crosse it. Let a man, in the choice of his meane, rather choose the fittest meane then the greatest meane; and rather them that deale in certaine things then those that are generall. The reparation of a Deniall is somtimes equall to the first Grant; if a man shew himselfe neither dejected nor discontented. *Iniquum petas ut æquum feras* is a good rule, where a man hath strength of Favour: but otherwise, a man were better rise in his Sute; for he that would have ventured at first to have lost the Sutour, will not in the conclusion lose both the Sutour and his owne former Favour. Nothing is thought so easie a request to a great Person, as his Letter; and yet, if it be not in a good cause, it is so much out of his reputation. There are no worse instruments then these generall contrivers of Sutes: for they are but a kinde of Poyson and Infection to Publique Proceedings.

Of Studies.

STUDIES serve for Delight, for Ornament, and for Ability. Their chiefe use for Delight is in privatenesse and retiring; for Ornament, is in discourse; & for Ability, is in the judgement and disposition of Businesse. For expert men can execute, & perhaps judge of particulars, one by one; but the generall counsels, and the plots, and marshalling of affaires, come best from those that are Learned. To spend too much time in Studies, is sloth; to use them too much for ornament, is affectation; to make judgement wholly by their rules is the humour of a Scholler. They perfect Nature, and are perfected by Experience: for naturall abilities are like naturall plants, that need proyning by Study: and Studies themselves doe give forth directions too much at large, except they be bounded in by experience. Crafty men contemne Studies; simple men admire them; and wise men use them: for they teach not their owne use; but that is a wisdome without them, and above them, won by observation. Reade not to contradict and confute; nor to beleeve and take for granted; nor to finde talke and discourse; but to weigh and consider. Some Bookes are to be tasted, others to be swallowed, and some few to be chewed and digested: that is, some Bookes are to be read onely in parts; others to be read but not curiously; and some few to be read wholly, and with Diligence and Attention. Some Bookes also may be read by deputy, and extracts made of them by others: but that would be onely in the lesse important arguments, and the meaner sort of Bookes, else distilled Bookes are like common distilled waters, flashy things.

Reading maketh a full man; Conference a ready man; and Writing an exact man. And therefore, if a man Write little, he had need have a great memory; if he Conferre little, he had need have a present wit; and if he Reade litle, he had need have much cunning, to seeme to know that he doth not. Histories make men wise; Poets witty; the Mathematicks subtill; Naturall Philosophy deepe; Morall grave; Logick and Rhetorick able to contend. *Abeunt studia in mores.* Nay there is no stond or impediment in the wit, but may be wrought out by fit Studies; like as diseases of the body may have appropriate exercises. Bowling is good for the stone and reines; Shooting for the lungs and breast; gentle Walking for the stomacke; Riding for the head; and the like. So if a man's wit be wandring, let him study the Mathematicks; for in demonstrations, if his wit be called away never so little, he must begin again: if his wit be not apt to distinguish or find differences, let him study the schoole-men; for they are *cymini sectores.* If he be not apt to beat over matters, and to call up one thing to prove and illustrate another, let him study the Lawyer's Cases: so every defect of the minde may have a speciall receit.

Of Faction.

MANY have an opinion not wise; that for a Prince to governe his Estate; or for a Great Person to governe his Proceedings, according to the respect of Factions, is a principall part of Policy: whereas contrariwise the chiefest wisdome is either in ordering those things which are generall, and wherein men of severall Factions doe nevertheless agree; or in dealing with correspondence to particular persons, one by one. But I say not that the consideration of Factions is to be neglected. Meane men, in their rising, must adhere; but great men, that have strength in themselves, were better to maintaine themselves indifferent and neutrall. Yet even in beginners, to adhere so moderately, as hee bee a man of the one Faction which is most passable with the other, commonly giveth best way. The lower and weaker Faction is the firmer in conjunction: and it is often seene that a few that are stiffe doe tire out a greater number that are more moderate. When one of the Factions is extinguished, the Remaining subdivideth: as the Faction betweene Lucullus and the rest of the Nobles of the Senate (which they called *Optimates*) held out a while against the Faction of Pompey and Cæsar: but when the Senate's authority was pulled downe, Cæsar and Pompey soone after brake. The Faction or partie of Antonius and Octavianus Cæsar, against Brutus and Cassius, held out likewise for a time; but when Brutus and Cassius were overthrowne, then soone after Antonius and Octavianus brake and subdivided. These examples are of warres, but the same holdeth in private Factions. And therefore, those that are seconds in Factions doe many times, when the Faction subdivideth, prove Principals: but many times also, they prove Ciphars and casheer'd: for many a man's strength is in opposition; and when that faileth he groweth out of use. It is commonly seene, that men once placed take in with the contrary Faction to that by which they enter; thinking belike that they have the first sure, and now are readie for a new purchase. The traitour in Faction lightly goeth away with it; for when matters have stucke long in ballancing, the winning of some one man casteth them, and he getteth all the thankes. The even carriage betweene two Factions proceedeth not alwaies of moderation, but of a truenesse to a man's selfe, with end to make use of both. Certainly in Italy they hold it a little suspect in Popes, when they have often in their mouth, *Padre commune:* and take it to be a signe of one that meaneth to referre all to the greatnesse of his owne House. Kings had need beware how they side themselves, and make themselves as of a Faction or Partie: for Leagues within the State are ever pernicious to Monarchies; for they raise an obligation, paramount to obligation of Soveraigntie, and make the King, *tanquam unus ex nobis:* as was to be seene in the League of France. When Factions are carried too high and too violently, it is a signe of weaknesse in Princes; and much to the prejudice both of their authoritie and businesse. The motions of Factions under Kings ought to be like the motions (as the Astronomers speake) of the inferiour Orbs; which may have their proper motions, but yet still are quietly carried by the Higher Motion of *Primum Mobile.*

❧ Of Ceremonies and Respects.

HE that is only reall had need have exceeding great parts of Vertue: as the stone had need to be rich, that is set without foile. But if a man marke it well, it is in praise and commendation of men as it is in Gettings and Gaines: for the Proverbe is true, *That light gaines make heavy purses:* For light Gaines come thick, whereas great come but now and then. So it is true, that small matters win great commendation, because they are continually in use, and in note: whereas the occasion of any great Vertue commeth but on festivals. Therefore it doth much adde to a man's reputation, and is (as Queene Isabella said) *like perpetuall letters commendatory*, to have good Formes. To attaine them, it almost sufficeth not to despise them; for so shall a man observe them in others; and let him trust himselfe with the rest. For if he labour too much to expresse them, he shall lose their Grace; which is to be naturall and unaffected. Some men's behaviour is like a Verse, wherein every syllable is measured: how can a man comprehend great matters, that breaketh his minde too much to small observations? Not to use Ceremonies at all is to teach others not to use them againe; and so diminisheth Respect to himselfe; especially they be not to be omitted to strangers, and formall natures; but the dwelling upon them, and exalting them above the Moone, is not only tedious but doth diminish the Faith and Credit of him that speakes. And certainly, there is a kinde of conveying of effectuall and imprinting passages, amongst complements, which is of singular use, if a man can hit upon it. Amongst a man's Peeres, a man shall be sure of familiaritie; and therefore it is good a little to keepe State. Amongst a man's Inferiours, one shall be sure of Reverence; and therefore it is good a little to be Familiar. He that is too much in any thing, so that he giveth another occasion of satietie, maketh himselfe cheape. To apply one's selfe to others is good; so it be with demonstration that a man doth it upon regard, and not upon facilitie. It is a good precept generally in seconding another, yet to adde somewhat of one's owne: as if you will grant his opinion, let it be with some distinction; if you will follow his motion, let it be with condition; if you allow his counsell, let it be with alledging further reason. Men had need beware how they be too perfect in Complements; for be they never so sufficient otherwise, their enviers will be sure to give them that attribute, to the disadvantage of their greater Vertues. It is losse also in businesse, to be too full of Respects, or to be too curious in observing times and opportunities. Salomon saith; *He that considereth the wind, shall not sow, and he that looketh to the clouds, shall not reape.* A wise man will make more opportunities then he findes. Men's behaviour should be like their Apparell, not too strait, or point device, but free for exercise or motion.

❧ Of Praise.

PRAISE is the reflection of Vertue. But it is as the glasse or bodie, which giveth the reflection. If it be from the common people, it is commonly false and naught: and rather followeth vaine persons, then vertuous: for the common people understand not many excellent Vertues: the lowest Vertues draw Praise from them; the middle Vertues worke in them Astonishment or Admiration; but of the highest Vertues, they have no sense or perceiving, at all. But shewes and *Species virtutibus similes* serve best with them. Certainly, Fame is like a River, that beareth up things light and swolne, and drownes things waighty and solide: but if persons of Qualitie and Judgement concurre, then it is (as the Scripture saith) *Nomen bonum instar unguenti fragrantis*. It filleth all round about, and will not easily away. For the odours of Oyntments are more durable then those of Flowers. There be so many false points of Praise, that a man may justly hold it a suspect. Some Praises proceed meerely of Flattery; and if hee be an ordinary Flatterer, he will have certaine common attributes, which may serve every man; if he be a cunning Flatterer, he will follow the Arch-flatterer, which is a man's selfe; and wherein a man thinketh best of himselfe, therein the Flatterer will uphold him most: but if he be an impudent Flatterer, look wherin a man is conscious to himselfe that he is most defective, and is most out of countenance in himselfe, that will the Flatterer entitle him to perforce, *Spreta conscientia*.

Some Praises come of good Wishes and Respects, which is a Forme due in Civilitie to Kings & Great Persons, *laudando præcipere;* when by telling men what they are, they represent to them what they should be. Some men are praised maliciously to their hurt, therby to stirre Envie and Jealousie towards them; *pessimum genus inimicorum laudantium;* in so much as it was a proverb amongst the Grecians; that he that was praised to his hurt, should have a push rise upon his nose: as we say, that a blister will rise upon ones tongue that tells a lye. Certainly moderate Praise, used with opportunity, and not vulgar, is that which doth the good. Salomon saith, *He that Praiseth his Frend aloud, rising early, it shall be to him no better then a curse.* Too much magnifying of man or matter doth irritate Contradiction, and procure Envie and Scorne. To praise a man's selfe cannot be decent, except it be in rare cases: but to praise a man's office or profession, he may doe it with good grace, and with a kinde of magnanimitie. The Cardinals of Rome, which are Theologues, and Friars, and Schoole-men, have a phrase of notable contempt and scorne towards civill businesse: For they call all Temporall Businesse of Warres, Embassages, Judicature, & other Emploiments, *Sbirrerie;* which is, *under-sheriffries;* as if they were but matters for Under-Sheriffes and Catchpoles; though many times, those Under-sheriffferies doe more good then their high speculations. St. Paul, when he boasts of himselfe, he doth oft enterlace; *I speake like a foole;* but speaking of his calling, he saith; *Magnificabo apostolatum meum.*

❧ Of Vaine-Glory.

IT was prettily devised of Æsope; *The Fly sate upon the Axle-tree of the Chariot wheele, and said, What a dust doe I raise?* So are there some Vaine Persons, that whatsoever goeth alone, or moveth upon greater means, if they have never so little Hand in it, they thinke it is they that carry it. They that are Glorious must needs be Factious; for all bravery stands upon comparisons. They must needs be Violent, to make good their owne Vaunts. Neither can they be Secret, and therefore not effectuall; but according to the French proverb; *Beaucoup de bruit, peu de fruit: Much bruit, little fruit.* Yet certainly there is use of this qualitie, in civill affaires. Where there is an opinion, and fame to be created either of vertue or greatnesse, these men are good Trumpetters. Again, as Titus Livius noteth, in the case of Antiochus, and the Ætolians; *There are sometimes great effects of crosse lies;* as if a man that negotiates between two Princes, to draw them to joyne in a Warre against the third, doth extoll the forces of either of them, above measure, the one to the other: and sometimes he that deales between man and man, raiseth his owne Credit with both, by pretending greater interest then he hath in either. And in these and the like kindes, it often falls out that Somewhat is produced of Nothing: for lies are sufficient to breed Opinion, and Opinion brings on Substance. In militar commanders and soldiers, Vaine-Glory is an essentiall point; for as iron sharpens iron, so by Glory one courage sharpneth another. In cases of great enterprise upon charge and adventure, a composition of Glorious Natures doth put life into businesse; and those that are of solide and sober natures, have more of the Ballast then of the Saile. In fame of learning, the flight will be slow without some feathers of Ostentation. *Qui de contemnenda gloria libros scribunt, nomen, suum inscribunt.* Socrates, Aristotle, Galen, were men full of Ostentation. Certainly Vaine-Glory helpeth to perpetuate a man's memory; and Vertue was never so beholding to humane nature, as it received his due at the second hand. Neither had the Fame of Cicero, Seneca, Plinius Secundus, borne her age so well, if it had not been joyned with some Vanity in themselves: like unto varnish, that makes seelings not onely shine, but last. But all this while, when I speake of Vaine-Glory, I meane not of that property that Tacitus doth attribute to Mucianus; *Omnium quæ dixerat feceratque Arte quadam Ostentator:* for that proceeds not of Vanity, but of naturall magnanimity and discretion: and in some persons is not onely comely, but gracious. For Excusations, Cessions, Modesty it selfe well governed, are but arts of Ostentation. And amongst those arts, there is none better then that which Plinius Secundus speaketh of; which is to be liberall of praise and commendation to others, in that wherein a man's selfe hath any perfection. For saith Pliny very wittily; *In commending another, you doe your selfe right; for he that you commend is either superiour to you in that you commend, or inferiour. If he be inferiour, if he be to be commended, you much more: if he be superiour, if he be not to be commended, you much lesse.* Glorious men are the Scorne of wise men; the Admiration of fooles; the Idols of parasites; and the Slaves of their own Vaunts.

❧ Of Honour and Reputation.

THE winning of Honour is but the revealing of a man's Vertue and Worth, without disadvantage. For some in their actions, doe wooe and affect Honour and Reputation. Which sort of men are commonly much talked of but inwardly little admired. And some, contrariwise, darken their Vertue in the shew of it; so as they be under-valued in opinion. If a man performe that which hath not beene attempted before; or attempted and given over; or hath beene atchieved, but not with so good circumstance; he shall purchase more Honour then by effecting a matter of greater difficulty or vertue, wherein he is but a follower. If a man so temper his actions, as in some one of them hee doth content everie faction or combination of people, the musicke will bee the fuller. A man is an ill husband of his Honour, that entreth into any action, the failing wherein it may disgrace him more then the carying of it through can Honor him. Honour that is gained and broken upon another hath the quickest reflection; like Diamonds cut with Fascets. And therefore let a man contend to excell any competitors of his in Honour, in out-shooting them, if he can, in their owne Bowe. Discreet followers and servants helpe much to Reputation: *Omnis fama a domesticis emanat.* Envy, which is the canker of Honour, is best extinguished by declaring a man's selfe in his ends, rather to seeke Merit then Fame: and by attributing a man's successes, rather to divine Providence and felicity, then to his owne vertue or policy. The true marshalling of the degrees of Soveraigne

Honour are these: In the first place are *Conditores Imperiorum;* founders of States and Common-Wealths: such as were Romulus, Cyrus, Cæsar, Ottoman, Ismael. In the second place are *Legis-latores*, Lawgivers; which are also called Second Founders or *Perpetui Principes*, because they governe by their ordinances, after they are gone: such were Lycurgus, Solon, Justinian, Eadgar, Alphonsus of Castile, the Wise, that made the *Siete Partidas*. In the third place, are *Liberatores* or *Salvatores:* such as compound the long miseries of civill warres, or deliver their countries from servitude of strangers or tyrants; as Augustus Cæsar, Vespasianus, Aurelianus, Theodoricus, K. Henry the 7. of England, K. Henry the 4. of France. In the fourth place are *Propagatores* or *Propugnatores Imperii;* such as in honourable warres enlarge their territories, or make noble defence against invaders. And in the last place, are *Patres Partiæ;* which reigne justly, and make the times good, wherein they live. Both which last kindes need no examples, they are in such number. Degrees of Honour in subjects are; first, *Participes Curarum;* Those upon whom Princes doe discharge the greatest weight of their affaires; their *Right Hands*, as we call them. The next are, *Duces belli*, great Leaders; such as are Princes' lieutenants; and doe them notable services in the warres. The third are, *Gratiosi;* Favourites; such as exceed not this scantling, to be solace to the Soveraigne, and harmelesse to the people. And the fourth, *Negotiis pares;* such as have great places under Princes, and execute their places with sufficiency. There is an Honour likewise, which may be ranked amongst the greatest, which happeneth rarely: that is, of such as sacrifice themselves to death or danger for the good of their countrey: as was M. Regulus, and the two Decii.

❧ Of Judicature.

JUDGES ought to remember that their office is *jus dicere*, and not *jus dare;* to Interpret Law, & not to Make Law, or Give Law. Else will it be like the authority claimed by the Church of Rome; which under pretext of exposition of Scripture doth not sticke to adde & alter; & to pronounce that which they doe not finde; and by shew of Antiquitie, to introduce noveltie. Judges ought to be more learned then wittie; more reverend then plausible; & more advised, then confident. Above all things, Integritie is their portion, and Proper Vertue. *Cursed* (saith the Law) *is hee that removeth the land-marke.* The mislaier of a meere stone is to blame. But it is the unjust Judge that is the capitall remover of land-markes, when he defineth amisse of lands and propertie. One foule sentence doth more hurt then many foule examples. For these doe but corrupt the Streame; the other corrupteth the Fountaine. So saith Salomon; *Fons turbatus, & vena corrupta, est justus cadens in causa sua coram adversario.* The office of Judges may have reference unto the Parties that sue; unto the Advocates that plead; unto the Clerkes and Ministers of Justice underneath them; and to the Soveraigne or State above them.

First, for the Causes or Parties that sue. *There be* (saith the Scripture) *that turne Judgement into Worme-wood;* and surely there be also that turne it into Vinegar; for Injustice maketh it bitter, and Delaies make it soure. The principall dutie of a Judge, is to suppresse Force and Fraud; whereof Force is the more pernicious when it is open; and Fraud when it is close and disguised. Adde thereto contentious suits, which ought to be spewed out, as the surfet of Courts. A Judge ought to prepare his way to a just sentence, as God useth to prepare his way, by raising valleys, and taking downe hills: so when there appeareth on either side an high hand, violent prosecution, cunning advantages taken, combination, power, great counsell, then is the vertue of a Judge seene, to make inequalitie equall; that he may plant his Judgement as upon an even ground. *Qui fortiter emungit, elicit sanguinem;* and where the wine-presse is hard wrought, it yeelds a harsh wine, that tastes of the grape-stone. Judges must beware of hard constructions and strained inferences; for there is no worse torture then the torture of Lawes. Specially in case of Lawes Penall, they ought to have care, that that which was meant for terrour be not turned into rigour; and that they bring not upon the people that shower whereof the Scripture speaketh; *Pluet super eos laqueos:* for penall lawes pressed are a *shower of snares* upon the people. Therefore let Penall Lawes, if they have beene sleepers of long, or if they be growne unfit for the present time, be by wise Judges confined in the execution; *Judicis officium est, ut res, ita tempora rerum, &c.*

In Causes of Life and Death, Judges ought (as farre as the law permitteth) in Justice to remember Mercy; and to cast a severe eye upon the example, but a mercifull eye upon the person.

Secondly, for the Advocates and Counsell that plead: Patience and gravitie of hearing, is an essentiall part of Justice; and an over-speaking Judge is no well tuned Cymball. It is no grace to a Judge, first to finde that which hee might have heard in due time from the Barre; or to shew quicknesse of conceit in cutting off evidence or counsell too short; or to prevent information by questions, though pertinent. The parts of a Judge in hearing are foure: To direct the evidence; to moderate length, repetition, or impertinency of speech; to recapitulate, select, and collate the materiall points of that which hath beene said; and to give the Rule or Sentence. Whatsoever is above these is too much; and proceedeth either of glory and willingnesse to speake; or of impatience to heare; or of shortnesse of memorie; or of want of a staid and equall attention. It is a strange thing to see that the boldnesse of Advocates should prevaile with Judges; whereas they should imitate God, in whose seat they sit; who *represseth the presumptuous*, and *giveth grace to the modest*. But it is more strange that Judges should have noted favourites; which cannot but cause multiplication of fees, and suspicion of by-waies. There is due from the Judge, to the Advocate, some commendation and gracing where Causes are well handled and faire pleaded; especially towards the side which obtaineth not; for that upholds in the Client the reputation of his Counsell, and beats downe in him the conceit of his Cause. There is likewise due to the Publique a civill reprehension of Advocates, where there appeareth cunning counsel, grosse neglect, slight information, indiscreet pressing, or an over-bold defence. And let not the Counsell at the Barre chop with the Judge, nor winde himselfe into the handling of the Cause anew, after the Judge hath declared his Sentence: but on the other side, let not the Judge meet the Cause halfe way; nor give occasion to the partie to say; *his counsell or proofes were not heard*.

Thirdly, for that that concernes Clerks and Ministers. The place of Justice is an hallowed place; and therefore not only the bench but the foot-pace and precincts and purprise thereof, ought to be preserved without scandall and corruption. For certainly, *Grapes* (as the Scripture saith), *will not be gathered of Thornes or Thistles:* Neither can Justice yeeld her fruit with sweetnesse, amongst the briars and brambles of catching and poling Clerkes and Ministers. The attendance of Courts is subject to foure bad instruments. First, certaine persons, that are sowers of suits; which make the Court swell and the Country pine. The second sort is of those that ingage Courts in quarells of Jurisdiction, and are not truly *Amici curiæ*, but *Parasiti curiæ;* in puffing a Court up beyond her bounds, for their owne scraps and advantage. The third sort is of those that may be accounted the left hands of Courts; persons that are full of nimble and sinister trickes and shifts, whereby they pervert the plaine and direct courses of Courts, and bring Justice into oblique lines and labyrinths. And the fourth is the poler and exacter of fees; which justifies the common resemblance of the Courts of Justice to the bush whereunto while the sheepe flies for defence in wether, hee is sure to loose part of his fleece. On the other side, an ancient Clerke, skilfull in presidents, wary in proceeding, and understanding in the businesse of the Court, is an excellent finger of a Court; and doth many times point the way to the Judge himselfe.

Fourthly, for that which may concerne the Soveraigne and Estate. Judges ought above all to remember the conclusion of the Roman Twelve Tables; *Salus Populi suprema Lex;* and to know that Lawes, except they bee in order to that end, are but things captious, and oracles not well inspired. Therefore it is an happie thing in a State when Kings and States doe often consult with Judges; and againe, when Judges doe often consult with the King and State: the one, when there is matter of Law intervenient in businesse of State; the other, when there is some consideration of State intervenient in matter of Law. For many times the things deduced to Judgement may bee *Meum & Tuum*, when the reason and consequence thereof may trench to point of Estate: I call Matter of Estate, not onely the parts of Soveraigntie, but whatsoever introduceth any great alteration or dangerous president; or concerneth manifestly any great portion of people. And let no man weakly conceive, that just Laws and true Policie have any antipathie; for they are like the spirits and sinewes, that one moves with the other. Let Judges also remember that Salomon's throne was supported by Lions on both sides; let them be Lions, but yet Lions under the throne; being circumspect, that they doe not checke or oppose any points of Soveraigntie. Let not Judges also be so ignorant of their owne right, as to thinke there is not left to them, as a principall part of their office, a wise use and application of Lawes. For they may remember what the Apostle saith of a greater Law then theirs; *Nos scimus quia Lex bona est, modo quis ea utatur Legitime.*

❧ Of Anger.

TO seeke to extinguish Anger utterly is but a bravery of the Stoickes. We have better oracles: *Be angry but sinne not. Let not the Sunne goe downe upon your Anger.* Anger must be limited and confined, both in race and in time. We will first speake how the naturall inclination and habit to be angry may be attempred and calmed. Secondly, how the particular motions of Anger may be repressed, or at least refrained from doing mischiefe. Thirdly, how to raise Anger or appease Anger in another.

For the first; there is no other way but to meditate & ruminate well upon the effects of Anger, how it troubles man's life. And the best time to doe this is to looke backe upon Anger, when the fitt is throughly over. Seneca saith well; *that Anger is like ruine, which breakes it selfe upon that it falls.* The Scripture exhorteth us *to possesse our soules in patience.* Whosoever is out of Patience, is out of possession of his Soule. Men must not turne Bees;

—animasque in vulnere ponunt.

Anger is certainly a kinde of basenesse: as it appeares well in the weaknesse of those subjects in whom it reignes: children, women, old folkes, sicke folkes. Onely men must beware that they carry their Anger rather with scorne then with feare: so that they may seeme rather to be above the injury then below it: which is a thing easily done, if a man will give law to himselfe in it.

For the second point; the Causes and Motives of Anger are chiefly three. First, to be too sensible of hurt: for no man is Angry that feeles not himselfe hurt: and therefore tender and delicate persons must needs be oft Angry: they have so many things to trouble them; which more robust natures have little sense of. The next is, the apprehension and construction of the injury offred, to be in the circumstances thereof, full of Contempt. For Contempt is that which putteth an edge upon Anger, as much or more then the hurt it selfe. And therefore when men are ingenious in picking out circumstances of Contempt, they doe kindle their Anger much. Lastly, opinion of the touch of a man's Reputation doth multiply and sharpen Anger. Wherein the remedy is, that a man should have, as Consalvo was wont to say, *telam Honoris crassiorem*. But in all refrainings of Anger, it is the best remedy to win time; and to make a man's selfe beleeve that the opportunity of his revenge is not yet come, but that he foresees a time for it; and so to still himselfe in the meane time, and reserve it.

To containe Anger from Mischiefe, though it take hold of a man, there be two things whereof you must have speciall caution. The one, of extreme Bitternesse of Words, especially if they be aculeate and proper; for *communia maledicta* are nothing so much; and againe, that in Anger a man reveale no secrets: for that makes him not fit for society. The other, that you doe not peremptorily break off, in any businesse, in a Fitt of Anger: but howsoever you shew bitternes, do not act any thing that is not revocable.

For raising and appeasing Anger in another; it is done chiefly by choosing of times, when men are frowardest and worst disposed, to incense them. Againe, by gathering (as was touched before) all that you can finde out to aggravate the Contempt. And the two Remedies are by the Contraries. The former to take good times, when first to relate to a man an Angry businesse; for the first impression is much : and the other is, to sever, as much as may be, the construction of the injury from the point of Contempt; imputing it to misunderstanding, feare, passion, or what you will.

❧ Of Vicissitude of Things.

SALOMON saith; *There is no new thing upon the earth.* So that as Plato had an imagination; *That all knowledge was but Remembrance:* So Salomon giveth his sentence; *That all noveltie is but Oblivion.* Whereby you may see that the river of Lethe runneth as well above ground as below. There is an abstruse Astrologer that saith; *If it were not for two things that are constant (the one is, that the Fixed Starres ever stand at like distance, one from another, and never come nearer together nor goe further asunder; the other, that the Diurnall Motion perpetually keepeth Time); no individuall would last one moment.* Certain it is, that the Matter is in a perpetuall flux, and never at a stay.

The great Winding-sheets that burie all things in oblivion, are two; Deluges and Earth-quakes. As for Conflagrations and great Droughts, they doe not meerely dispeople and destroy. Phaeton's carre went but a day. And the three yeares' drought in the time of Elias was but particular, and left people alive. As for the great Burnings by Lightnings, which are often in the West Indies, they are but narrow. But in the other two destructions, by Deluge and Earth-quake, it is further to be noted, that the remnant of people which hap to be reserved, are commonly ignorant and mountanous people, that can give no account of the time past: so that the oblivion is all one, as if none had beene left. If you consider well of the people of the West Indies, it is very probable that they are a newer or a younger people then the people of the

Old World. And it is much more likely that the destruction that hath heretofore been there, was not by Earth-quakes, (as the Ægyptian priest told Solon concerning the island of Atlantis; *that it was swallowed by an Earth-quake*); but rather that it was desolated by a particular Deluge. For Earth-quakes are seldome in those parts. But on the other side, they have such Powring Rivers, as the rivers of Asia, and Affrick, and Europe are but brookes to them. Their Andes likewise, or mountaines, are farre higher then those with us; whereby it seemes that the remnants of generation of men were in such a particular Deluge saved. As for the observation, that Macciavel hath, that the jealousie of sects doth much extinguish the memory of things; traducing Gregory the Great, that he did what in him lay to extinguish all Heathen Antiquities; I doe not finde that those zeales doe any great effects, nor last long: as it appeared in the succession of Sabinian, who did revive the former Antiquities.

The Vicissitude or Mutations in the superiour globe are no fit matter for this present argument. It may be, Plato's great Yeare, if the world should last so long, would have some effect; not in renewing the State of like individuals (for that is the fume of those that conceive the Celestiall Bodies have more accurate influences upon these things below then indeed they have), but in grosse. Comets, out of question, have likewise power and effect over the grosse and masse of things: but they are rather gazed upon, and waited upon in their journey, then wisely observed in their effects; specially in their respective effects; that is, what kinde of Comet, for magnitude, colour, version of the beames, placing in the region of Heaven, or lasting, produceth what kinde of effects.

There is a Toy, which I have heard, and I would not have

it given over, but waited upon a little. They say it is observed in the Low Countries (I know not in what part) that every five and thirtie years the same kinde and sute of years and weathers comes about againe; as great frosts, great wet, great droughts, warme winters, summers with little heat, and the like; and they call it the Prime. It is a thing I doe the rather mention, because computing backwards, I have found some concurrence.

But to leave these points of Nature, and to come to Men. The greatest Vicissitude of things amongst men is the Vicissitude of Sects and Religions. For those orbs rule in men's minds most. The true Religion is *built upon the rocke;* the rest are tost upon the waves of time. To speake, therefore, of the causes of new Sects; and to give some Counsell concerning them; as farre as the weaknesse of humane judgement can give stay to so great revolutions.

When the Religion formerly received is rent by discords; and when the holinesse of the professours of Religion is decayed and full of scandall; and withall the times be stupid, ignorant, and barbarous; you may doubt the springing up of a New Sect; if then also there should arise any extravagant and strange spirit, to make himselfe authour thereof. All which points held when Mahomet published his Law. If a New Sect have not two properties, feare it not: for it will not spread. The one is the supplanting or the opposing of Authority established: for nothing is more popular then that. The other is, the giving licence to pleasures and a voluptuous life. For as for Speculative Heresies (such as were in ancient times the Arrians, and now the Arminians), though they worke mightily upon men's wits, yet they doe not produce any great alterations in States; except it be by the helpe of civill occasions. There be three manner of plantations of New Sects. By the power of Signes and Miracles: by the eloquence and wisedome of Speech and Perswasion: and by the Sword. For Martyrdomes, I reckon them amongst Miracles; because they seeme to exceed the strength of human nature: and I may doe the like of superlative and admirable holinesse of life. Surely there is no better way to stop the rising of New Sects and Schismes then to reforme abuses; to compound the smaller differences; to proceed mildly, and not with sanguinary persecutions; and rather to take off the principall authours by winning and advancing them, then to enrage them by violence and bitternesse.

The Changes and Vicissitude in Warres are many: but chiefly in three things; in the seats or stages of the Warre; in the weapons; and in the manner of the conduct. Warres in ancient time, seemed more to move from East to West: for the Persians, Assyrians, Arabians, Tartars (which were the invaders), were all easterne people. It is true, the Gaules were westerne; but we reade but of two incursions of theirs; the one to Gallo-Grecia, the other to Rome. But East and West have no certaine points of Heaven: and no more have the Warres, either from the East or West, any certainty of observation. But North and South are fixed: and it hath seldome or never been seene that the farre Southern People have invaded the Northern, but contrariwise. Whereby it is manifest that the Northern tract of the world is in Nature the more martiall region: be it in respect of the Stars of that Hemisphere, or of the great Continents that are upon the North; whereas the South Part, for ought that is knowne, is almost all Sea; or (which is most apparent) of the cold of the Northern parts, which is that which, without aid of discipline, doth make the bodies hardest, & the courages warmest.

Upon the Breaking and Shivering of a great State and Empire, you may be sure to have Warres. For great Empires, while they stand, doe enervate and destroy the forces of the natives which they have subdued, resting upon their owne protecting forces: and then when they faile also, all goes to ruine, and they become a Prey. So was it in the decay of the Roman Empire; and likewise, in the Empire of Almaigne, after Charles the Great, every bird taking a fether; and were not unlike to befall to Spaine, if it should break. The great accessions and unions of Kingdomes doe likewise stirre up Warres. For when a State growes to an over-power, it is like a great floud, that will be sure to overflow. As it hath been seene in the states of Rome, Turky, Spaine, and others. Looke when the world hath fewest barbarous peoples, but such as commonly will not marry or generate, except they know meanes to live (as it is almost every where at this day, except Tartary), there is no danger of inundations of people: but when there be great shoales of people, which goe on to populate, without foreseeing meanes of life and sustentation, it is of necessity that once in an age or two they discharge a portion of their people upon other nations: which the ancient Northern People were wont to doe by lot; casting lots what part should stay at home, and what should seeke their fortunes. When a warre-like State growes soft and effeminate, they may be sure of a Warre. For commonly such States are growne rich in the time of their degenerating; and so the prey inviteth, & their decay in valour encourageth a Warre.

As for the Weapons, it hardly falleth under rule and observation: yet we see even they have returnes and vicissitudes. For certain it is, that Ordnance was known in the City of the Oxidrakes in India; and was that which the Macedonians called Thunder and Lightning, and Magicke. And it is well knowne that the use of Ordnance hath been in China above 2000 yeares. The conditions of Weapons, and their improvement are; First, the fetching a farre off: for that outruns the danger: as it is seene in Ordnance and Muskets. Secondly, the strength of the percussion; wherin likewise Ordnance doe exceed all arietations and ancient inventions. The third is, the commodious use of them; as that they may serve in all wethers; that the carriage may be light and manageable; and the like.

For the Conduct of the Warre: at the first, men rested extremely upon Number: they did put the Warres likewise upon Maine Force, and Valour; pointing dayes for pitched fields, and so trying it out upon an even Match: and they were more ignorant in Ranging and Arraying their Battailes. After they grew to rest upon Number, rather competent then vast: they grew to advantages of place, cunning diversions, and the like: and they grew more skilful in the ordering of their Battailes.

In the youth of a State, Armes doe flourish: in the middle age of a State, Learning; and then both of them together for a time: in the declining age of a State, Mechanicall Arts and Merchandize. Learning hath his infancy, when it is but beginning and almost childish; then his youth, when it is luxuriant and juvenile; then his strength of yeares, when it is solide and reduced; and lastly, his old age, when it waxeth dry and exhaust. But it is not good to looke too long upon these turning wheeles of Vicissitude, lest we become giddy. As for the Philology of them, that is but a circle of tales, and therefore not fit for this writing.

A FRAGMENT OF AN ESSAY.

Of Fame.

THE poets make Fame a Monster. They describe her in part, finely & elegantly; and in part, gravely & sententiously. They say, look how many Feathers she hath, so many Eyes she hath underneath: so many Tongues; so many Voyces; she pricks up so many Ears. This is a Flourish: there follow excellent Parables; as that she gathereth strength in going; that she goeth upon the ground and yet hideth her head in the clouds. That in the day time she sitteth in a Watch Tower, and flyeth most by night: that she mingleth things done with things not done: and that she is a terrour to great Citties: but that which passeth all the rest is: they do recount that the Earth, mother of the Gyants, that made war against Jupiter and were by him destroyed, thereupon in an anger brought forth Fame: for certain it is, that Rebels, figured by the Gyants, and Seditious Fames, and Libels, are but brothers and sisters; masculine and feminine. But now, if a man can tame this Monster, and bring her to feed at the hand, and govern her, and with her fly other ravening fowle and kill them, it is somewhat worth. But we are infected with the stile of the poets. To speak now in a sad and serious manner: there is not, in all the politiques, a Place lesse handled and more worthy to be handled then this of Fame. We will, therefore, speak of these points. What are false Fames; and what are true Fames; and how they may be best discerned; how Fames may be sown, and raised; how they may be spread and multiplyed; and how they may be checked and layed dead. And other things concerning the nature of Fame. Fame is of that force, as there is scarcely any great action wherein it hath not a great part; especially in the War. Mucianus undid Vitellius by a Fame that he scattered; that Vitellius had in purpose to remove the legions of Syria into Germany, and the legions of Germany into Syria: whereupon the legions of Syria were infinitely inflamed. Julius Cæsar took Pompey unprovided, and layed asleep his industry and preparations by a Fame that he cunningly gave out; how Cæsar's own souldiers loved him not; and being wearied with the wars, and laden with the spoyles of Gaul, would forsake him as soon as he came into Italy. Livia setled all things for the succession of her son Tiberius by continuall giving out that her husband Augustus was upon recovery and amendment. And it is an usuall thing with the Basshawes, to conceale the death of the Great Turk from the Jannizaries and men of war, to save the sacking of Constantinople and other towns, as their manner is. Themistocles made Zerxes, king of Persia, poast apace out of Græcia by giving out that the Græcians had a purpose to break his bridge of ships, which he had made athwart Hellespont. There be a thousand such like examples; and the more they are, the lesse they need to be repeated; because a man meeteth with them every where. Therefore, let all wise Governers have as great a watch and care over Fames as they have of the Actions and Designes themselves.

[*The rest was not finished.*]